The Business of Diversity

A View from the Corporate Suite

Youlanda M. Gibbons

Georgetown University

cognella™
San Diego, CA

First published in the United States of America in 2011 by Cognella, a division of University Readers, Inc.

Trademark Notice: Product or corporate names may be trademarks or registered trademarks, and are used only for identification and explanation without intent to infringe.

15 14 13 12 11   1 2 3 4 5

Printed in the United States of America

ISBN: 978-1-60927-821-2

www.cognella.com   800.200.3908

Shekinah Glory

Contents

Acknowledgments

In completing this book, I have many debts to acknowledge. Conversations resulting in inspiration, encouragement, new perspectives, and prayers have all played their part in helping me to think clearly about this work. Special thanks to my students, colleagues, friends, and family for our many discussions regarding this book.

Special thanks to those who taught me sociology—for imparting an enduring enthusiasm for the discipline. The questions that you have posed have challenged me to provide answers that show the exciting nature of sociology as a systematic method of revealing facts that are explainable and illustrative. I am grateful to those whose curiosity has pointed me in the direction that they found interesting and significant. Many thanks to those whose books on various aspects of sociology have helped me think better about how to make sociological theory and research more accessible and applicable to others.

I would like to particularly thank Sharon Hermann, Jennifer Bowen, Lionel D. Scott, Jr., and Amy Hemmati for their assistance with editing and providing substantive feedback on my work. I am most grateful to Elizabeth Fitzpatrick, my editor's editor, for your meticulous work in the final stages of this book project. Special thanks to Elizabeth Harrison Hicks for your significant reviews and guidance of appropriate style, clarity, and presentation. To Brenda Girton-Mitchell, thank you for your kindness and generous spirit as you have helped to develop within me a sense of authority and humility. And to Sonya Reeves for continuously asking the right question, thank you. To my parents, Mildred and Wilson Gibbons, thanks for loving, caring, and providing for me throughout this project.

It is with a warm heart that I owe much gratitude and appreciation to Melvin Maxwell for lifting me and this work to the glory of God. Without the encouragement and well-informed comments of Melvin, this book would not have taken the form that it has. It is a pleasure to acknowledge the help he has given, as well as his spiritual guidance.

Preface

Just as many other higher education institutions, the University of Massachusetts–Amherst responded to the "affirmative action crisis" and the recurring debates over gender and race policies by eliminating affirmative action preferences across its business units. However, what was most disturbing and perplexing personally was the action undertaken by the university to change the name of the its Office of Equal Opportunity and Affirmative Action. Today, the title reads "Office of Equal Opportunity and *Diversity*."

Like the university, I wondered if other work organizations were replacing the language of *affirmative action* with *diversity*. What did this mean *really*? How does an organization *do* diversity? What motivates or influences organizations to enact diversity? How do organizations enact diversity? What are the key features or characteristics of organizations that tend to enact diversity? And are diversity behaviors within the organizations actually new and improved versions of affirmative action practices?

When turning to the sociological and organization research literature, I was dismayed to discover that there was *very* little evidence that addressed my questions. In fact, my search of the scholarly and popular literature on diversity in organizations revealed a growing body of research on how workplace diversity is *theorized*. Most studies attempt to apply the concept of diversity as a framework for analyzing political power, language structures, social identity, cultural values, intergroup relations, and discrimination.

This research project sought *not* to provide evidence of how diversity is conceptualized, but rather *how it is implemented* in the corporate sector. This focus is important, given the degree to which *talk* of diversity in organizations has pervaded the vast majority of corporations, colleges and universities, federal agencies, and nonprofit organizations. As argued by Jacoby (1994), workplace diversity may have become somewhat of an organizational and educational buzzword, signifying everything, anything—and nothing. The American notion to *embrace* diversity has become a fashionable dimension of many organizations, and as a result, has exerted pressures to implement diversity strategies and programs.

My motivation to conduct research in this area was fueled by the fact that the rise of diversity as corporate strategy occurred at a time when support for affirmative action and civil rights laws pertinent to the workplace was under great scrutiny. During this time, corporate messages of *valuing diversity, encouraging inclusion, managing diversity, retaining diversity, supporting diversity,* and *fostering diversity* tend to reflect a recent way of thinking about not only employees, but customers and the global economy as well.

The linkage between *valuing* and *incorporating* diversity is essential. Today, the majority of scholarly research on diversity in organizations fails to provide evidence of this linkage. It is my aim to provide evidence of how *valuing diversity* translates into diversity behaviors within one of the nation's most critical, innovative, and globally dependent employment industries—the Information Technology Sector.

Chapter One

The eagle, soaring, clear-eyed, competitive, prepared to strike, but not a vulture. Noble, visionary, majestic, that people can believe in and be inspired by, that creates such a lift that it soars. I can see that being a good logo for the principled company. Okay, guys, enough bullshit.

—Ira Jackson, Dean of Claremont University
Peter F. Drucker and Masatoshi Ito
Graduate School of Management

Chapter One
Women and Minorities: An Untapped Resource in the Global Economy

I have always been enamored of corporations. They wield great power, money, and resources. As such, they are positioned to make a significant impact on societies. Corporations, whether they are good or bad, shape societies. Their influence goes beyond the board room, as corporations shape and drive legislation on myriad issues including regulation, medical and technological research, tax structures, and education. Often beloved for what they do and hated for what they do not do, corporations are a viable part of American life that lead us to some unexpected ways of understanding the relationships among labor, gender, and race.

The relationships among labor, race, and gender are inextricably linked to corporate structures and behaviors. Specifically, policies, practices, strategies, and activities represent how the corporation functions. It is within the constraints of these mechanisms that we gain a fuller understanding of how labor calls for a capacity to deal with people. In a world that is filled with swift and increasing demographic change, corporations are shifting attention to new and emerging markets. Accompanying this change is an expansion into the world's labor market. In the United States, women and minorities are becoming increasingly desired populations for the new and improved global workforce.

Women, minorities, and the American corporation—it is an old issue, but one that is still very much alive. It has new nuances and insights. With nearly fifty years of experience of recruiting and hiring women and minorities, much can be explored to determine why and how corporations seek out women and minority talent. Amidst social forces, both external and organizational, corporations continue to grapple with the issue of women and minorities in the firm. Examining corporate structures and behaviors is a good way to discover why and how companies respond to and interpret their labor needs of women and minorities. Why and how do these groups fit into the existing structures and behaviors of the firm?

Since the early 1990s, American corporations have been fascinated with what is termed "diversity." Companies throughout the country have instituted and jumped on the diversity bandwagon. A decade and a half ago, "fierce" and "bold" characterized corporations' actions about diversity. It was not uncommon to pick up the *Wall Street Journal, Fortune 500,* or *Forbes* and see a front-page article on diversity in American corporations. Strange, somewhat—what is going on in corporate America to allow for such a watershed of support of diversity at this period in America's history? In fact, what is going on in American society to substantiate such support of diversity? These basic questions allow us to give pause to American corporations.

It is then important to determine what motivates their behavior to adopt and implement diversity strategies to pursue women and minorities. In what ways do they seek out and retain these groups? Do corporations experience challenges or frustrations when they pursue women and minorities, and are there implications for these experiences? The search for answers to these questions leads to two distinct discussions: one concerning the influence of the external environment; and the other leading to a discussion of organizations' arrangements and behaviors.

In describing why and how corporations adopt and implement diversity strategies, I have drawn on empirical and interview data from a random sample of information technology corporations from across the country. When considering the type of industry that might be struggling to find qualified women and minorities, those related to science and engineering came to mind. Over the past several decades, the nation has called attention to the underrepresentation of women and minorities in science and engineering. What better sector to explore in terms of its diversity efforts? However, it is important to gain more than an elementary insight into the nation's information technology sector and its needs and conditions for labor. As the IT sector expands and continues to flourish, I consider how its growth affects the trajectory of corporation's perspectives on women and minorities as employees.

National reports suggest that the information technology sector in the United States is a key pillar of the U.S. economy. It is attractive, prevalent, and dynamic. It continues to attract the attention of investors and federal agencies looking to transfer information quickly, safely, and accessibly. Information technology is regarded as an engine of growth and rapid change across the global economy. A growing body of literature suggests that information technology is driving national productivity. Many researchers agree that no one could predict the pace of progress in the information technology sector. Twenty years ago, computing was associated with stand-alone business systems involving an enormous amount of processing. Now, digital technologies are bountiful and powerful. They have transformed computing into batch processing, batch processing into time-sharing, time-sharing into personal computing, and, as of late, personal computing into information appliances connected to the Internet (National Research Council 2001). Beginning with the "supercomputer" to servers to desktops to portables, information technology has captured the imagination, creativity, productivity, and profitability of nearly every industry in the U.S. economy. The almighty "microprocessor" has changed fundamentally the ways in which people interact, communicate, conduct business, and produce and access information.

Taking into account the sector's slowdown (resulting from an economic recession) from the end of 2000 into 2002, information technology intensive industries, namely software, computer, and telecommunications services, have enjoyed substantial growth. Information technology spans manufacturing, administrative, and technical workforces. This translates into an incredible feature of the information technology sector—it has the capacity to be expansive and it thereby encompasses a wide range of services. For example, the information technology employment market is no longer restricted to providing employment opportunities to individuals with purely technical backgrounds. For every computer programmer there are likely a number of project managers, systems analysts, customer support and account managers, technical managers, sales mangers, trainers, educators, and even non-IT market employees. The incredible growth and profitability of this sector has also impacted non-profit and community organizations, which have benefited greatly from the philanthropy of both information technology corporations and individuals. Microsoft Corporation is a prime example.

As noted by the National Research Council (NRC), the perception of rates of rapid growth contributes significantly to the sense of urgency that characterizes the information technology sector. In IT-intensive industries, talk of competitive pressures and the need to be continuously innovative is related to the objective to be first to market a product. Because product innovation depends absolutely on the talents of people, the information technology sector is also characterized as labor intensive. This means that the supply of well-trained and highly qualified employees is essential. During the 1990s, corporate actions such as alliances, mergers, and acquisitions created a heightened demand for information technology employees with specialized skills and work experience. In essence, this workforce laid the groundwork for the growth of the global corporations that continue to dominate the industry. Data from this period provide historical context for the current IT workforce and has remained consistent for the past decade.

In 1997 the first study was released by the Information Technology Association of America (ITAA), claiming that the nation is experiencing a significant shortage of information technology employees in large and mid-sized U.S. companies. Based on a larger sample one year later, the ITAA published another report indicating an even more serious shortage of information technology employees. Skeptics of the "projected" information technology labor shortage, such as the General Accounting Office, questioned ITAA's methodology and provided compelling evidence that there really was no labor shortage. Organizations and individuals quickly weighed in on the debate and arguments that immediately began to surface around proposed legislation to issue H-1B visas that were awarded instantly to foreign prospective information technology employees.

By the mid 1990s, information technology companies began to hire foreign workers because of their expressed difficulty of locating well-trained and highly qualified Americans. Critics responded by claiming that the primary reason information technology companies were remotely interested in foreign talent was the financial incentives associated with foreign labor. Put simply, foreign information technology talent was believed to be less costly than domestic labor.

Although during the past few years much attention has been focused on foreign labor in the information technology sector, other sources of potentially qualified labor should not go unrecognized. It is true that empirical evidence indicates that women and minorities are severely underrepresented in information technology-related fields. In 1997, only 27 percent of U.S. computer and mathematical scientists were women. Only 4 percent were African American and 3 percent were Latino, while 12 percent were Asian American. According to the National Science Board (2000), in 1986, 36 percent of earned baccalaureate degrees in computer science went to women; a decade later, the proportion declined to 28 percent. The numbers of women earning master's degrees in computer science also declined from 30 percent in 1986 to 26 percent in 1996.

Often, science and engineering talent can be traced back to an individual's academic and recreational experiences during the elementary and middle school years. Research reported by the NRC indicates that elementary and middle school boys and girls were using computer games and the Internet in roughly equal proportions. High school males and females were also roughly equal in their use of the computer. Although high school females have increased their participation in science, only 17 percent of all students taking advanced placement courses in computer science in 1997 were female.

According to the National Science Board (2000), 33 percent of African American and Latino college freshmen anticipated majoring in science and engineering in 1998. This percentage was slightly higher than the percentage of white students choosing these areas of study (30 percent). However, the percentage of white and Latina women anticipating majoring in science and engineering was substantially smaller. The gap between men and women was largest among white and Latino students—ten- and nine-point gaps, respectively. The gap was smallest among African American students—32 percent of females versus 34 percent of males anticipated majoring in science and engineering. More significantly, a number of education reports show a substantive decline or drop-off between freshmen's declarations of their intent to study science and engineering and the actual completion of a science or engineering degree. Underrepresented U.S.-born African Americans and Latinos are more likely not to earn science and engineering degrees within five years compared to their white counterparts. A higher proportion of these groups tend to change their majors to those in non-science and non-engineering fields.

During the 1980s and 1990s, the percentages of racial and ethnic minorities receiving baccalaureate degrees in science and engineering increased slightly. However, these numbers remain at low levels. Among U.S. minority citizens and permanent residents awarded a B.S. degree in mathematics and computer science, 10 percent were African American, 5 percent were Latino, and less than one half of 1 percent were Native American or Alaskan Native. For master's degrees, minority proportions were even lower: Fewer than 6 percent were African American, 3 percent were Latino, and 0.3 percent were Native American or Alaskan Native (National Science Board 2000). However, to gain more insight into the differences in the proportion of minorities and whites receiving college-level degrees in science and engineering, it is important to consider the role of historically black colleges and universities (HBCUs) in attracting and retaining students in scientific and engineering disciplines.

First, there is empirical evidence that compares differences in the number of science and engineering graduates in HBCUs and majority institutions. According to data collected by the National Science Foundation over the past two decades, on average, HBCUs granted twice the number of degrees in computer science than did majority institutions. The National Science Foundation claims that the large number of students attending majority institutions who are attracted to and express an interest in science and engineering disciplines do not complete their degrees in such fields. Therefore, explanations for the difference in the number of science and engineering degrees granted to whites and African Americans in both types of institutions lies *not* in the academic profiles of their students—for example, those who express an interest, declare a major, or earn a degree in science and engineering—but rather in the ways in which the *institutions* attract and retain students in these disciplines.

To understand what HBCUs might be doing differently to attract and retain minority students in science and engineering, it is useful to consider the "pipeline model" and how it affects students' demonstration of scientific knowledge. According to the NRC, when implementing the pipeline model in majority institutions, students permeate certain barriers designed to filter out those who are incapable of attaining the next levels of scientific knowledge. Those students who remain are expected to enter and "fit" into the scientific and technical professions.

The model employed in the HBCU is quite different. Instead of placing an emphasis on "filtering" students, the HBCU model stresses *inclusion* or pooling of students. Extensive outreach, mentoring, and support are key elements. Creating a supportive environment within the institution, as well as among peers, results in students not fending for themselves, but when expressing academic difficulties, being offered intellectual, emotional, and academic support. Also, studies indicate that the HBCU model is effective in attracting and retaining women in science and engineering majors, especially the mentoring component.

For those earning college and university degrees in a science or engineering discipline, as is the case for most majors, upon graduation, employment opportunities are desired. The information technology labor force looks favorable. The US Department of Commerce has a forecast of the 30 fastest growing professional occupations between 2008 and 2018. The second fastest growing jobs are Network Systems and Data Communications Analyst, projected to grow at 53.4 percent. Also included in the top 25 fastest growing jobs are Computer Engineers for Application at 34 percent growth and Systems Software at 30.4 percent growth.

Clearly, the nation's imperative to strengthen its technological workforce and its scientific talent pool has profound implications when considering the underrepresentation of women and minorities. This has been described as a *serious* issue by the nation's leading researchers and business and education leaders. The National Science Foundation has recently adopted this issue as a priority, placing special emphasis on the underrepresentation of women and minorities in the information technology workforce.

Having a grasp of the future of the nation's information technology workforce is important. Data collected on the number of women and minorities in the technology workforce suggest that African Americans, Latinos, and women are an entire pool of talent that remains untapped.

Professionals in information technology industries reflect neither the demographics of today's population nor those projected in the future. According to the NRC's report *Building a Workforce for the Information Economy*, the information technology workforce is predominantly white, male, young, and educated. Although this workforce is becoming more diverse in terms of race, ethnicity, and nation of birth, it is less so with regard to gender.

In 2009, whites dominated the information technology workforce by representing 72.6 percent of all workers. Asian and Pacific Islanders represented 17 percent, whereas African Americans represented 6.1 percent, and Latinos represented 5 percent. No data is available for Native Americans during 2009.

It is clear that the information technology workforce is overwhelmingly male. 75 percent of the workforce in 2009 was male. Although the majority of the information technology workforce is US-born, the proportion of foreign-born individuals rose from 13 percent in 1995 to 22 percent in 2009. By comparison, all foreign-born workers constitute about 10 percent of employees in the United States. In terms of educational levels, about two-thirds of the information technology workforce between 1995 and 1999 had at least a bachelor's degree, compared to about one-third of all employed individuals, and three-fourths of all employed in professional specialty occupations in the United States.

Research Study

By applying appropriate organization-environment perspectives, the intention of my research is to investigate why and how information technology corporations adopt diversity strategies geared toward women and minorities. Three and a half years of collecting empirical and interview data is sufficient time in which to document some of the perceptions, challenges, and frustrations experienced by corporations as they establish and implement diversity strategies. These experiences are circumscribed by economic, political, and social forces and pressures. Focusing on corporate policies, practices, activities, and behaviors, rather than on women and minority perceptions of diversity strategies, seems to be the best way to draw attention to the particularities of why and how corporations do diversity.

My primary thesis is that information technology corporations adopt diversity strategies because of interpretation of interorganizational ties, legal mandates and political pressures, human resources professionals, and internal, formal labor market practices. To test my thesis, I gathered data from a mail survey questionnaire sent to a randomly selected group of one hundred information technology corporations. Information was also generated from a select group of eighty human resources professionals. Interview subjects were individuals employed in the one hundred corporations participating in the mail survey questionnaire (See Research Method). In order to gain a better understanding of organization features that characterized participating information technology corporations, survey data indicate a general profile of corporations in terms of employee racial and gender composition, company size, age, location, revenue volume, and industry type by the presence of diversity strategies (see Appendix A for a complete listing of corporations and profiles of participating corporations).

My survey questionnaire (see Appendix B–*Organizational Responses to Diversity: A Survey of the Nation's Information Technology Employers*) focused on corporations' experiences with recruitment, hiring, and retention activities targeting U.S.-born women and minorities, namely African Americans, Asian Americans, Latinos, and Native Americans. It was necessary to create questions that would encourage corporations to begin and continue to the end. In this regard, questions were presented in an order of sequence to ensure a sense of logic and clear understanding of the purpose of the study. To provide consistency throughout the questionnaire, the format of closed-ended questions with ordered-answer choices was employed to address anticipated time constraints of informants. Dillman (2001) suggests that this format can yield concise, usable, and cost-effective responses. A few open-ended important questions were included in the questionnaire, such as "What is your company's statement on diversity?" and "What is your company's age?"

After pre-testing the survey questionnaire several times, it was mailed out to a random sample of information technology intensive corporations across the United States. Three waves of mailings yielded a total of one hundred completed, usable survey questionnaires. Survey data analyses were straightforward. Simple descriptive statistics were employed to describe the relevant characteristics and compare important factors associated with the adoption of diversity strategies. Because my emphasis was on predictors of the adoption of diversity strategies, multivariate regression analyses were employed. The overall goal of both descriptive and multivariate analyses was to determine the structure and behavior of corporations that adopt diversity strategies.

The survey questionnaire method was supplemented by in-depth, semi-structured interviews (see Appendix C–*Executives and Senior Managers Interview Protocol*). I employed two interview techniques. They were the key informant and narrative methods. Kahn and Cannell (1957, 57) describe in-depth interviewing as "a conversation with a purpose." Data generated from key informant interviews and narratives offered a clearer and better understanding of the questionnaire data. Themes and patterns that emerged from interviews were relevant to my research questions and hypotheses. In fact, results from the survey questionnaire alone could not have been interpreted easily or have provided rich explanations. Indeed, interview data were necessary to meet the goal and objectives of my research.

I conducted and structured interviews in terms of the research objective—to investigate why and how information technology corporations adopt diversity strategies. As argued by Whyte (1984), the nature and structure of the key informant interview is not fixed by predetermined questions, but rather is designed to provide the respondent with the freedom to introduce materials or information that were not anticipated by the interviewer. Because many interview subjects in my study were employed in positions characterized by excessive work loads and tight schedules, it was necessary to develop a set of very broad, semi-structured questions that would ultimately address time constraints yet yield the best possible information.

The key informant interview method rests on the assumption that in order to understand the *shaping* of individuals' attitudes, we must probe for reports of experiences. Moreover, the first step toward this objective is to describe the *events* the subject has experienced that are most relevant to one's study. When the interview is focused on events as revealed by the informant, Whyte argues that we can gain a better understanding of informant attitudes if we link them with the events experienced.

Because my research focus is on corporate structures and behaviors and not on the human resources professional specifically, I chose a rather informal sampling approach for interview subjects. The process of selecting human resources professionals was based on convenience. As prospective interview subjects, I chose human resources professionals who offered further assistance toward the completion of my research. Individuals who wrote encouraging notes and attached business cards to the returned survey questionnaire were considered as potential interview subjects. Human resources professionals who established contact by telephone or electronic mail to inform me that they were in the midst of completing the questionnaire or to request additional time were also identified as potential key informants. Finally, I considered human resources professionals employed by the top-ranked information corporations in the U.S. and abroad. These interview subjects were of particular interest given their corporation's high visibility and large employee size. In any case, these criteria were convenient given that the survey questionnaire sampling procedure provided no contact names.

Interview subjects held the job titles of vice president, senior manager, regional or district manager, director, and senior consultant. They were located in and reported usually to one or two divisions within the corporation—human resources management and legal areas. In some cases, interview subjects were located in the Office for Diversity, considered to be its own department in the corporation. Surprisingly, after a week or so of receipt of the letter of invitation to participate in my study, the vast majority of subjects agreed to provide an interview. In general, they were college-educated and middle-aged and, on average, had been employed in the human resources profession for fifteen to twenty years. Subjects' average age was forty-six at the time of the interviews. Nearly half of the interview subjects were women and one-fifth identified as an ethnic minority. At the time of the interviews, two-thirds of the subjects were employed in a Fortune 500 corporation. In terms of U.S. regional location, the majority of subjects were located in the corporation's headquarters or primary site. Interview subjects were employed in corporations spanning thirty to one hundred nine years in operation. Industry types embraced three broad areas of information technology—manufacturing, software development and programming, and telephone and communications services.

Once my interview subjects understood the goals of my research, they were quite generous with their time and even welcomed the opportunity to provide their insights and experiences as key players in their corporations. On average, interviews were ninety minutes long but no shorter than fifty minutes. In fact, I found that the majority of the interview responses were quite honest and sought to illuminate many of the challenges and difficulties associated with the pathways and barriers to attracting and retaining women and minority talent.

Many interview subjects seized the opportunity to provide clarification and interpretation of misunderstood popular notions of "diversity" behaviors in corporate America. In each interview, I paid close attention to common and different themes as subjects told of their experiences in working with corporate leadership, colleagues in their departments, and external organizations such as colleges and universities. By sharing their experiences and perspectives on why and how diversity behaviors exist or fail to exist in their company, different events and occurrences came together. I found that the key informant method triggered reflection in many of the interview subjects and was of great value.

On an interesting note, many of my peers cautioned that members of the business community, especially those in large corporations, may be less inclined to participate in the interview process because of their busy schedules. Also, it was suspected that prospective interviewees, given their key positions within the company, might be consumed with serious work challenges and responsibilities associated with major lay-offs and hiring freezes influenced by the nation's economic recession. Of major concern, my peers predicted that given the focus of my research, much of the interview data would resemble what they called public relations or "PR spill." They asserted that my interviews more than likely would yield public opinion and attitudes about diversity rather than the corporation's honest views and practices concerning diversity. After all, the PR spill's primary concern is creating and maintaining a positive image through effective communications. I found just the opposite.

Data generated from both key informant and narrative interviews were used to relate practice to theory (the reality of social phenomena). In this context, descriptive data were summarized then linked to more general theoretical constructs presented throughout this book. As a method of illustration, interview data were employed in my research to build upon theory by drawing on substantive data generated from human resources professionals located in America's leading information technology corporations.

Both survey and interview data provide important knowledge and information concerning corporations' structures and behaviors associated with the recruitment, hiring, and retention of women and minorities. As such, these data offer a broader view and understanding of the influence of the environment on corporations' decision making and strategic choices. Although quite powerful, resourceful, and resilient, corporations, too, are impacted by social forces. My research shows how over the last few decades, significant change has occurred in the life span of the corporation that ultimately impacts their interests and motivation to adopt and implement diversity strategies.

Themes of Analyses

Chapter 2 begins by placing corporate diversity strategies in a socio-historical context by examining the history and legacy of civil rights in America and its impact on the creation and implementation of equal employment laws and practices. This chapter focuses on changes in political action over time, political-economic structures, and dominant ideologies that give shape to these changes. Chapter 2 then shifts to the role of corporations in reinventing equal employment opportunity practices such as Affirmative Action programs into diversity structures and behaviors. A look at empirical research on the impact of diversity on organization performance provides an understanding of the relevance of diversity initiatives in work organizations. This chapter further points to the complexities that underlie diversity strategies that address inequality and inclusion in the workplace.

Corporations' insistence on the difficulty in hiring women and minority scientists and engineers sets the stage for Chapter 3. Identifying specific challenges and conditions that plague corporations in their pursuit of talent allows for an in-depth exploration of commonly held beliefs about a massive labor shortage in the information-technology sector. This chapter also suggests that there are certain industry types more prone to experience difficulty in hiring women and minorities. In addition to a description of common barriers and challenges to entry into the information-technology sector, a discussion of alternative strategies to hiring women and minorities is provided. Chapter 3 also deals with the issue of outsourcing, in the context of hiring foreign workers as a threat to hiring U.S.-born women and minority talent. As a significant way of averting barriers to entry, this chapter discusses the role of diversity strategies in hiring well-trained and highly qualified women and minority talent.

Chapter 4 is about corporations' perceptions of legal mandates, court judgments, and political pressures to adopt and implement diversity strategies. Corporations' attitudes toward the importance of the relationship between Affirmative Action, Equal Employment Opportunity, and diversity are explored. Are Affirmative Action practices the same as implementing diversity strategies? Do diversity strategies go well beyond Affirmative Action practices?

The argument that corporations implement diversity strategies because of past injustices and inequality is also discussed in Chapter 4. The contention that corporations implement diversity strategies as a means of reducing vulnerability to and risk of legal sanctions and accusations of discrimination implies that diversity structures and behaviors serve as defenders of the corporation. This chapter also offers an extensive discussion on the role and impact of H-1B visas on securing information technology professionals as it relates to the recruitment and hiring of women and minority talent.

Chapter 5 takes a look at the relationship between corporations and women and minority organizations. Recently, establishing and maintaining relationships with historically black colleges and universities and women and minority science and engineering associations have proven ineffective in recruiting and hiring women and minority talent. In fact, HBCUs are becoming less and less important as a primary supplier of women and minority talent. This chapter claims that many women and minority organizations' primary function with corporations is to serve as recipients of financial contributions and sponsorships. However, the tide has shifted. Corporations are seeking out alternative ways of recruiting women and minorities. No longer are HBCUs the leading vehicle for securing a diverse workplace.

In Chapter 6, I bring the firm in. In other words, attention is now focused on the organization and its arrangements. Corporations that adopt and implement diversity strategies *justify* them. They do not create and absorb them without rationale. This chapter discusses how business, moral, and pluralistic arguments underscore a corporation's decision to adopt strategies targeted toward women and minorities. Customers, markets, population, and workplace demographics, past inequality and injustice, social legitimacy, and public opinion give shape to the policies and practices that embody why and how corporations seek strategies to recruit, hire, and retain women and minorities.

The challenge of getting and keeping women and minority professionals is addressed in Chapter 7. I discuss a number of factors related to the successful hiring and retention of women and minorities and the adoption of diversity strategies. First, a critical mass of women and minority professionals is associated with the presence of corporate diversity strategies. Second, most relevant to corporations' decisions to adopt and implement diversity strategies is leadership. Without the involvement and endorsement of senior managers and executives, diversity strategies lack accountability and are vulnerable to being reduced to symbolic gestures and corporate rhetoric.

Third, I also explore the relationship between traditional hiring- and retention-type strategies on the presence of women and minorities. I provide a discussion focused on how performance, supervision, mentoring, executive leadership programs, and rotating job assignments are positively associated with women and minorities' long-term employment with the corporation.

In Chapter 8, I propose four imperatives of diversity that motivate corporations to adopt diversity strategies. The enforcement, moral, business, and pluralistic imperatives encourage corporations to implement structures and behaviors geared toward women and minorities. Often combined and integrated, the imperatives reflect the primary structures and behaviors of corporations. They move corporations to be responsive to environmental and organizational change. In this view, the enforcement, moral, business, and pluralistic imperatives of diversity are vehicles by which strategies are created and applied to the unique needs and conditions of women and minorities. In this chapter, I also discuss how corporations that adopt diversity strategies tend to demonstrate certain priorities. These priorities are foundational to our understanding of the enforcement, moral, business, and pluralistic approaches to "doing diversity."

Finally, in Chapter 9, the book's conclusion, I pull together the important threads that illustrate why and how information technology corporations develop and implement diversity strategies. I provide a synthesis of major themes running throughout previous chapters while offering a rich and substantive discussion of why and how organizational arrangements contribute to the presence of women and minorities.

I highlight the primary arguments that give shape to the enforcement, moral, business, and pluralistic imperatives of diversity in Chapter 9. I also tackle the complications, challenges, and struggles that corporations identify as indicative to "doing diversity." Central to my argument is that, indeed, there are certain reasons corporations focus recruitment, hiring, and retention strategies on women and minorities. However, I argue that there is variation among corporations in their efforts in doing so. The environment and organization arrangements shape the corporations' views on the relevance of women's and minorities' presence in the firm. What then continues to shape these corporate views is essential to women and minorities who seek entry to this sector and who are likely to benefit from its continued success as a major driving and innovative force in the global economy.

Chapter Two

What strange bedfellows: civil rights, affirmative action, reverse discrimination and diversity! Did they ever have anything to do with each other?

—Youlanda Gibbons, Professor of Sociology
and Liberal Studies, Georgetown University;
Diversity and Inclusion Consultant, NASA

Chapter Two
The Hammer and the Velvet Glove of Diversity

Yesterday did mean something! To understand the connections between diversity, markets, legal mandates, and corporations, one must consider the great political and social transformation that forced corporations to realize that a diverse workforce would be good for business. A grasp of the significance of diversity in organizations begins with the civil rights movement and the emergence of diversity ideology in American businesses.

The legal and legislative "hammer" approach is marked by the nation's experiences of peril and persistence to achieve workplace equality. However, changing conventional wisdom that the "hammer" approach fails to achieve economic success has led American corporations to create opportunity structures that employ a softer, gentler "velvet glove" approach, emphasizing strategy rather than compliance. Sociologist Frederick Lynch's 1997 seminal work *The Diversity Machine* characterizes diversity in American corporations. It provides an analysis of how diversity ideology has surfaced in two directions: first, as manifested as internal tensions between certain groups, such as those who promote diversity as a continuance of the civil rights movement; and second, as represented by those who view diversity as a good business strategy that ultimately improves the corporation's bottom line. Diversity, be it viewed as a newly improved version of American civil rights or a set of innovative and competitive business practices, has manifested itself in organizational practices and behaviors.

Although there is no definitive number on how many U.S. corporations have developed and implemented diversity strategies, researchers estimate the number at more than 70 percent (Winterle 1992; SHRM 1995; Wheeler 1995; Mueller 1996). Common among these initiatives are the creation of diversity action plans, the endorsements of diversity in mission statements from senior level management, the implementation of diversity training programs, and the establishment of diversity task force groups and councils. Providing the breath of life to these diversity initiatives are powerful constituents such as chief executive officers, presidents and chancellors of colleges and universities, nonprofit organizations, government agencies, research institutions, and philanthropic organizations, including public and private foundations.

The persistence of organizational behaviors grappling with diversity is due, at least in part, to the way in which it is linked to the notion of morality and corporate responsibility. The United States discrimination laws imply a strong sense of a moral imperative to right the wrongs of society. This is demonstrated mostly in corporations' aims to persistently correct past racial and ethnic injustices, in particular. These efforts are most noticeable in their mission statements, official reports, and formal documents. In most cases, these statements use the word "diversity" and tend to attach the principles of equality, nondiscrimination, fairness, and justice. Here are some examples:

- **General Motors**. "Many people, one GM, Now. At GM, we are striving to create and maintain an environment that naturally enables the people of General Motors, its unions, suppliers, and dealers to fully contribute and achieve personal fulfillment in the pursuit of total customer enthusiasm."

  Official GM Statement on Diversity

- **Exxon Mobil**. "We strive to attract the *best* talent available to meet our business requirements. As a result, we have built a diverse worldwide workforce with a common focus on attaining superior business results. We must continue to foster an environment that values the wide range of perspectives inherent in our diverse workforce, encourages individual growth and achievement, and rewards employees based on their performance and contribution to the realization of business objectives. This cannot be accomplished aggressively. It requires the active, ongoing commitment of all Exxon Mobil employees. Only when every employee feels fully valued and fully utilized, will we achieve our competitive potential. Maintaining our position as the world's premier petroleum and petrochemical company depends on our steadfast commitment to this endeavor."

Lee R. Raymond, Chairman and CEO

- **General Electric**. "I want to make sure GE is always the employer of choice. This has got to be a place where the best people want to come to work and where they want to stay and they come here because we do leading edge work. We allow people to live their dreams in an open and fair, diverse environment. We treat everybody with respect; the best get paid like the best in a performance culture. If having a meritocracy is incredibly important to your culture and what you believe in, diversity is the manifestation that says that everybody, no matter what their background, can excel in this company and so I just believe within my soul that diversity is incredibly important."

Jeff Immelt, Chairman and CEO

- **International Business Machines (IBM) Corporation**. "… to provide equal opportunity and affirmative action for applicants and employees, IBM carries out programs on behalf of women, minorities, people with disabilities, Vietnam-era veterans, Special Disabled Veterans […] this includes outreach as well as human resources programs that ensure equity in compensation and opportunity for growth and development […] managers are expected to ensure a work environment free of all forms of discrimination and harassment."

Official IBM Statement on Diversity

- **AT&T Corporation.** "As a global company touching diverse customers and markets wherever we do business, AT&T values individual perspectives. We recognize that it is just and right to treat every human being and their culture with decency and respect. First and foremost of Our Common Bond values is 'respect for individuals.' It is the foundation of our other values—helping customers, adhering to the highest standards of integrity, innovation and teamwork—and central to leveraging the dimensions of diversity."

  Official AT&T Statement on Diversity

- **United States Postal Services**. "The Postal Services requires new thinking and new structures that regards Diversity Development as fundamental to business success to achieve our corporate strategic goals. Diversity is that which makes each of us unique. It can be our birthplace, education, age, gender, neighborhood, race, social class, economic status, values, skills, appearance, lifestyle, etc. Valuing diversity is accepting and appreciating people's uniqueness. Developing diversity involves building tools and nurturing a culture that fully understands uniqueness and talent to support other organization goals."

  Robert Harris, VP of Diversity

- **Merrill Lynch Corporation**. "Merrill Lynch is committed to ensuring that diversity thrives at every level and at every location of our company. In the words of Chairman and Chief Executive Officer David H. Komansky, 'We must constantly work to create an environment at Merrill Lynch where a diversity of cultures, people, and ideas provide a catalyst for professional and personal achievement.' As Merrill Lynch has successfully reinvented itself over the years—from a U.S.-based retail securities broker to a diversified global financial services company—our workforce diversity efforts have evolved as well. Our focus on race and gender issues that has driven our program and policies since we began our diversity initiatives in the United States in 1992 has broadened to include a global perspective. In one of our five guiding principles—Respect for the Individual—our diversity imperative is to create a corporate environment that promotes mutual respect, acceptance, cooperation, and productivity among people from varying backgrounds. To achieve this, we are working to weave our policies into the very fabric of Merrill Lynch—at every level, across every business unit, and in all our business."

Official Merrill Lynch Statement on Diversity

Often referring to the racial and gender composition of an organization, diversity brings with it a complexity of political, legal, cultural, moral, and social issues. For the most part, diversity in an organizational context is influenced greatly by external factors, including projections of changes in workplace demographics, the demonstrated and visible commitment of senior management, legal mandates and regulatory pressures, vulnerability and risk of discrimination and sexual harassment lawsuits, and the heightened awareness of corporate responsibility. In these cases, an organization's motivation for adopting and implementing diversity strategies is a matter of historical reference and pressure from powerful social forces. Of equal importance is what is frequently cited as the business case of diversity. Put another way, the corporation's bottom line—its profits. However, what is central to these explanations is something much more fundamental—that which drives the corporation to adopt diversity-related strategies is their understanding of the history of race relations and gender politics in American society. This is an important place to begin. This history commences with the administration of civil rights laws and their application to corporate America.

Civil Rights Legislation in the 1960s and 1970s

Lynch (2001) provides an exceptional chronology of the political and legal history of diversity in the United States. The focus here is an understanding of how certain events contributed to the emergence and adoption of diversity behaviors in American corporations. From 1961, when President John F. Kennedy created the Presidential Committee on Equal Employment Opportunity, to 1990, when the Americans with Disabilities Act was enacted, the United States has implemented laws against the discrimination of historically oppressed groups—women, minorities, and people with disabilities. Over the past forty years, the nation has seen the passage of the Equal Pay Act of 1963, the 1964 Civil Rights Act, the Age Discrimination Act of 1976, and the Pregnancy Discrimination Act of 1978.

This time period also bore the passage of the Equal Employment Opportunity Act (EEO) and President Kennedy's Executive Order No. 10925, later reaffirmed by President Lyndon Johnson's Executive Order No. 11246, commonly known as Affirmative Action (AA). Although most corporations use the terms Equal Employment Opportunity and Affirmative Action interchangeably, there is an important difference. The Equal Employment Opportunity law states that discrimination is illegal and organizations shall *not* discriminate. Conversely, Affirmative Action directives dictate remedies or resolutions for named groups, indicating that organizations shall compensate for past discrimination and injustices.

Civil rights legislation of the 1960s sought to eliminate discrimination and racism by simply making illegal discrimination practices and behaviors within work organizations. Originating in the civil rights movement of the 1960s, Title VII of the 1964 Civil Rights Act prohibited employers from discriminating on the basis of sex, race, national origin, or religion. In response to this law, the Equal Employment Opportunity Commission (EEOC) was created to investigate allegations or charges of workplace discrimination and solve such disputes through administrative action in federal court.

During the late 1960s, addressing and elaborating on enforcement rules of Title VII and Affirmative Action, the United States Department of Labor targeted federal contractors. This group was directed to implement "affirmative action" for one reason—to correct past injustices and discrimination. At first, the actual meaning of affirmative action was quite vague and required business and industry to make a "reasonable" effort to create a more diverse workforce. But later, this directive, as interpreted and implemented by corporate managers, would seek to remedy the proportional imbalances between federal contractors' workforce composition and that of the general population labor pools. Hence, goals and timetable formulas, often referred to today as "quotas," were established to ensure that certain groups, that is, women and minorities, were not underused. In order to minimize the risk of court judgments or negative legal consequences, many employers began to adopt voluntary affirmative action plans to address the proportional racial and gender imbalances in the workplace (Lynch 1997). Not surprisingly, corporations used Affirmative Action principles and sentiments for their own self-interests, acting on an obligation to their shareholders. To reduce the possibility of lawsuits or boycotts or to capitalize on untapped human resources, the American corporation will use important aspects of the social and political environment to survive. In fact, it is dependent upon them to do so.

When I think about the 1960s and early 1970s, I remember what I've learned about these times (I was born in 1968). They were characterized by urban unrest, racial riots, and the emergence of militant and black power movements such as the Black Panthers. These protests forced corporations to recognize the consumer and labor powers held by organized groups of minorities and address the stark reality of a racially divided workforce. Ultimately, such social unrest added to the necessity of implementing Affirmative Action for the inclusion of minorities in the national workforce. As a method of forestalling racial conflict and tension, the nation's political and economic elites would begin the widespread implementation of Affirmative Action, thus making it a part of the day-to-day operations in the American workplace. In essence, the nation's key political players wanted peace.

Infrequently acknowledged, the role of Affirmative Action in ensuring and advancing equality in the workplace is credited to President Richard Nixon, not President John Kennedy. It was during the Nixon administration that equal employment laws gained much substance and momentum. Although Equal Employment Opportunity laws existed, during the early 1970s many corporations failed to continue to implement policies or programs to address discriminatory hiring practices. It was during this time that Nixon's Department of Justice began to establish stringent enforcement measures by directing the EEOC to bring lawsuits against corporations that were not incorporating antidiscrimination practices into their business structures and behaviors. Over the next several years, the EEOC would take many of the nation's largest corporations to court. AT&T, General Motors, and Sears were among them.

By 1975, nearly every major U.S. corporation had established an Equal Employment Opportunity compliance office, they had hired an Equal Employment Opportunity compliance officer, and some corporations established special positions to promote and hire minorities only (Thomas 1999). By the late 1970s, the EEOC began to shield employers implementing voluntary Affirmative Action programs from reverse discrimination allegations and complaints.

Over the next decade the U.S. Supreme Court would transform Affirmative Action. The *Griggs v. Duke Power* case specifically forced corporations to address "diversity" from a business perspective. Thirteen black men at the Duke Power Company who were required to pass a high school equivalency test to be considered for promotions filed a lawsuit that would take them all the way to the Supreme Court. The court unanimously ruled that business could not test applicants for jobs or promotions in a way that restricted opportunities for blacks. In their opinion, the court contended that employees are required to pass tests related to their actual job qualifications. Not surprisingly, in the aftermath of *Griggs*, many corporations eliminated general aptitude tests and others compared test scores with individuals of the same race (Wood 2003).

In June 1979, the Supreme Court continued to weigh in on the issue of race and employment in the *Weber v. Kaiser Aluminum & Chemical Corporation and United Steelworkers of America* case. Brian Weber, a white worker at the Louisiana factory at Kaiser Aluminum, sued the corporation because he claimed that he had been passed over for promotion due to the company's Affirmative Action practices. By a ruling of 5-2, the court established a company's right to use voluntary Affirmative Action programs that excluded white males. This ruling gave corporations the constitutional right to use racial preferences and quotas in hiring in order to overcome imbalances in the workplace, even if the corporation had not demonstrated a history of racial discrimination. Little did Weber know that his case would trigger a watershed of allegations of reverse discrimination in the courts over the next three decades.

In the 1977 case *Fullilove v. Klutznick*, the Supreme Court ruled 6-4 that Congress acted constitutionally in setting aside 10 percent of government contracts for minority-owned businesses involving a $4 billion public works program. However, most scholars agree that the political winds of Affirmative Action began to shift as the Reagan administration blew through Washington and overhauled each branch of government. In 1983, the court considered a case brought by a group of white police officers and firefighters that challenged the constitutionality of a lower court order that favored blacks and Latinos in the case of layoffs. With a 6-3 margin in *Firefighters Local Union No. 1784 v. Stotts*, the higher court ruled in favor of the firefighters, contending that the lower court exceeded its power when it required that white employees be laid off in a seniority system where blacks possessed less seniority. Although recognized as a small victory, *Firefighters Local Union No. 1784 v. Stotts* alerted the business community that the Reagan administration was not a friend to Affirmative Action.

The Transformation of Affirmative Action

During the Reagan-Bush administrations, the Republican Party paved the way for the opponents of "racial and gender preferences." Considered a worthy debate, the political majority opposed racial and gender preferences in any format, especially Affirmative Action. Opposition to Affirmative Action was a national platform agenda item for a decade. In 1985, Attorney General Edwin Meese put forth the motion to rewrite Executive Order 11246, the source of Affirmative Action programs, and make goals and timetables voluntary and not mandated under U.S. law (Lynch 1997). However, Meese met with great opposition.

Not only were civil rights advocates up in arms, but the business community was as well. Corporations asserted that Affirmative Action goals and timetables were good for the bottom line. This political retreat from Affirmative Action goals would tarnish the relationship between the administration and major corporations. In response to such strong opposition, the Reagan administration conducted a survey of one hundred twenty-seven large corporations. They were asked if they were planning to continue to use numerical objectives to track the progress of women and minorities in their corporation *regardless* of government mandates. Ninety-five percent of the corporations surveyed indicated "yes." Given the influence and lobbying power of the almighty corporation, in 1986 and 1987, the U.S. Supreme Court upheld forms of "quotas" as established by the U.S. Department of Labor.

When examining the proportions of political appointments by race and gender, George H. W. Bush has been praised for including a historical number of women and minorities in his administration. However, history shows that most crucial and fierce attacks on Affirmative Action occurred during the same period. Signing the 1991 Civil Rights Act in the midst of the Clarence Thomas hearing and refusing to sign a directive by C. Boyden Gray to eliminate racial preferences in federal employment raised great concern for civil rights advocates. In fact, many would agree that these two actions fueled yet again the nation's preoccupation with race and gender in the workplace. It was during the 1990s that many conservative Americans assumed that Affirmative Action programs no longer embodied the early ideals of color-blind nondiscrimination. Rather, the strong belief that Affirmative Action represented blatant gender and racial proportionalism and reverse discrimination would resound throughout all levels of most work organizations (Lynch 1997).

The Backlash of Affirmative Action

Nearly twenty-five years after the initial implementation of Affirmative Action practices in the corporate sector, many Americans believed that the time had come to put an end to such efforts. However, it was difficult to find opponents of Affirmative Action arguing *against* diversity and inclusion. Sociologist Nathan Glazer published in 1975 the first book in opposition to Affirmative Action, *Affirmative Discrimination: Ethnic Identity and Public Policy.* This work proposes that Affirmative Action practices are a form of discrimination against white males and as a result are a barrier to fairness and equality in the promotion and hiring processes for white males. Glazer suggests that minorities who are less qualified than white males are circumventing better-qualified whites for jobs. These assertions would mark the beginning of much criticism to come during the 1980s and 1990s.

Immersed in great ambivalence and criticism, Affirmative Action opponents sprang up by leaps and bounds throughout the 1990s. A wealth of widely cited works such as books and articles attacked the principles and spirit of Affirmative Action programs. Authors such as Charles Murray, Frederick Lynch, and William Beer claimed that Affirmative Action unfairly denied equal opportunity and gave preference to the *less* qualified by putting forth the foundations of merit, fairness, and reverse discrimination. Interestingly, a few distinguished minority authors were among the critics as well. Thomas Sowell, Shelby Steele, Roosevelt Thomas, Linda Chavez, and Clarence Thomas provided compelling arguments against Affirmative Action. These authors claimed that Affirmative Action placed an unfair burden on minorities, de-emphasizing their achievements and accomplishments. They agreed that Affirmative Action failed to improve the quality of life for the masses of minorities still living in poverty.

The contentious debate concerning Affirmative Action tends to center on the effects of its programs. For example, Roosevelt Thomas argues that Affirmative Action's achievements have been "stupendous," whereas A. W. Blumrosen maintains that neither supporters nor opponents give nondiscrimination laws much credit for their effectiveness. Nonetheless, in general, there is a wealth of inconsistent findings on the impact of AA programs. For example, In 1991, Uri and Mixon found that between 1972 and 1980, federally enacted Affirmative Action programs had a profound impact on the increased economic mobility of African Americans. On the other hand, examining employment data between 1947 and 1988, women between the ages of twenty and fifty-four began to lose gains in employment stability between 1981 and 1988. It is important to note that these were the Reagan administration years. Likewise, Sharon Collins, in 1989, found that between 1980 and 1985, there was a reduction on the focus of EEO and Affirmative Action as defined by the responsibilities of Affirmative Action corporate executives.

Most importantly, at the center of the Affirmative Action backlash was this notion of reverse discrimination. As a concept, reverse discrimination was propositioned by leading scholars and supported by many individuals who were members of the powerful and political elite. Reverse discrimination is closely associated with the U.S. Supreme Court decision *Regents of California v. Bakke*. As mentioned earlier, this ruling held that the university could give lawful consideration to race in future admissions procedures. This ruling continues to ignite the grand debate between those who argue that Affirmative Action represents reverse discrimination and those who argue that it does not. Over the past few years, American colleges and universities have had a defining role in the Affirmative Action controversy. In *Hopwood v. the State of Texas*, the plaintiff was denied admission to the University of Texas Law School although she alleges she was better qualified than several African American and Mexican American students who were admitted. The U.S. Court of Appeals ruled that the admissions procedure was unconstitutional given that three separate admissions councils were used to render decisions—one representing each racial group. This decision, however, did not change the ruling that race can be used as a factor in the selection and admissions procedures. However, a striking blow against Affirmative Action occurred in 1995. The Board of Regents in the State of California voted to eliminate the use of "race, gender, religion, color, ethnicity, or nationality" as criteria in its admission decisions and in hiring and contracting decisions. During this time, the California Board of Regents directed university officials to develop a policy that would "ensure that the student body remains diverse." This was a popular example of an institution that recognized the importance of diversity, to the extent that they implemented institutional diversity-driven structures independent of federal mandates.

The next several years proved to be a battleground in the United States Supreme Court with Affirmative Action at its center. Two lawsuits would prompt the nation to rethink its position on Affirmative Action and higher education. In June 2003, the Supreme Court decided that the *Grutter v. Bollinger* case upheld the principles that underlined the *Bakke* decision. The Court upheld the University of Michigan's Law School decision to use race as a factor in the admissions decisions process. Two years later, in a separate case challenging the University of Michigan's undergraduate admissions policies, the Supreme Court continued to uphold the right of universities to consider race in admissions procedures in order to achieve a diverse student population. Given its vicious attacks, these victories were considered a victory for Affirmative Action.

Whether a positive or negative force, the ends of Affirmative Action tend to justify its means. Its practices have paved the way for organizations, especially corporations, to redirect and refocus their level of commitment to ensuring equality in the workplace. Some proponents of Affirmative Action claim that many Americans abandoned its ideals in favor of diversity. The ideological sentiments during the Reagan-Bush years shifted the tide away from a kinder and gentler nation to a colder and less socially responsible nation. Civil rights advocates and supporters were greatly concerned that the government had essentially reversed its stance on racial inequality. At the same time, factors such as mergers, acquisitions, downsizing, and a slowing economy pushed corporate executives to develop "bottom-line justifications" for diversity. In the face of severe criticism, court battles, and the softening of government mandates such as Equal Employment Opportunity and Affirmative Action, corporate leaders sought to maintain their commitment to diversity in the workplace through its business goals and objectives.

Indeed, the backlash of Affirmative Action practices has spilled over into American corporations. This backlash has contributed to the adoption of corporate diversity strategies. In essence, the spirit of diversity grew during the decline of support for Affirmative Action throughout the United States. Broadening its reach, diversity, unlike Affirmative Action, became the *desired* choice for providing equal employment opportunity for women and minorities. The criticism of Affirmative Action made way for diversity strategies purposed to continuing to pursue and retain women and minorities without the baggage that Affirmative Action sentiments tend to bring.

Diversity as Corporate Strategy

Yet, there is another important motivator for adopting diversity strategies—the Hudson Institute's report *Workforce 2000*. This report is perhaps one of the most commonly cited and frequently referenced concerning the need for corporations to adopt diversity strategies. *Workforce 2000* identified the changing racial and gender composition of the nation's workforce, proclaiming that by the year 2000, 85 percent of new workers would be women and minorities. This startling statistic influenced corporate leaders' decisions to make diversity a bottom-line issue.

As argued by Yakura (1996, 42), the assumptions that underlie diversity bring a new set of ideals that "lie uncomfortably on top of the Equal Employment Opportunity and Affirmative Action debates." In contrast to Equal Employment Opportunity and Affirmative Action mandates, diversity assumptions differ remarkably given their emphasis on recognizing the uniqueness of individuality as opposed to homogenized equality and neutrality. The corporation's potential to enhance performance and increase creativity among its employees justifies and is dependent on its diversity efforts. After all, competition and profit become the impetus for valuing and investing in *everyone's* potentialities regardless of racial, class, and gender group membership.

Unlike Equal Employment Opportunity and Affirmative Action practices, in theory, Yakura states that diversity efforts are attractive and easily defensible. For example, at the individual level, the principle of diversity rests on the premise that the individual, not the group, has the opportunity to demonstrate his or her potential. In this view, the image of the white male being edged out begins to fade and is replaced by an image of a work environment where everyone can be successful, hence leading to the enhanced performance and profitability of the entire organization.

In terms of the effect of diversity on organization performance, at the time of this writing, there exist a few large-scale studies. Rosabeth Kanter's 1984 article *The Change Masters* encompasses a large sample of organizations providing evidence that corporations with progressive human resources management have enjoyed profitability over two decades. The second study, focusing on race and gender exclusively, Heidrick and Struggles' *The New Diversity: Women and Minorities on Corporate Boards* found that companies with two or more women or two or more minority directors on their corporate board are more likely to be listed on *Fortune* magazine's *Most Admired Companies* list. Likewise, in 1993, the *Wall Street Journal* reported results from a study indicating that corporations that have demonstrated a good record of recruiting and retaining women and minorities have stock prices nearly 10 percent higher than corporations with poor recruitment and retention records. And, lastly, by examining the relationship between diversity and financial performance in the food industry, Hayden and colleagues in 1994 found that corporations with the best diversity programs also were the best financially performing firms.

But as is the case with Affirmative Action, critics of diversity have emerged and have become quite vocal. Many Americans claim that by focusing on diversity, with its emphasis on the individual and inclusion, the Affirmative Action debate is ignored. As suggested by Robert Jackall, diversity is interpreted as "window dressing" for the interests of white males while being perceived as serving the interests of women and minorities by perpetuating "token" inclusion. Critics of diversity advance that organizations use diversity rhetoric as a means of shielding themselves against potential discrimination lawsuits rather than as a mechanism for ensuring equal opportunity. To the extent possible, diversity's symbolic behaviors serve as distractions from addressing the discriminatory patterns in hiring and promotion practices. In a popular article in *Black Enterprise* (July 2002), diversity is scrutinized *because* of its efforts to create an inclusive work environment. Critics argue that as African Americans become more and more of a minority among other ethnic groups, there is a need for standard, metropolitan statistical analysis. When assessing the ethnic and gender profile of a geographic location, the purpose of such analysis is to determine what the metric should be, as a template, when comparing it to the overall demographic composition of an organization. In this view, some African American leaders suggest that it is probable that diversity and inclusion efforts might *exclude* significant portions of African Americans.

Undoubtedly, there is great complexity underlying Equal Employment Opportunity, Affirmative Action, diversity, and their relationship to each other. This complexity lies in the values that we, as individuals, as groups, and as a nation, hold deeply and dear. Yet, in certain instances, the values that influence our notions of equality and fairness often lead us to reconsider and re-examine what they mean. History reminds us that at the heart of these value-based considerations are enduring racial and gender issues.

Recognizing this complexity, my research aim here is not to determine the best practice or ideological approach for addressing workplace inequality or discrimination, nor is it to investigate women's and minorities' perceptions of workplace discrimination. Rather it is to explore and explain those salient factors associated with diversity structures and behaviors in the corporate setting, that is, the environment and organization influences that motivate the adoption of diversity strategies. I offer a better understanding of the conditions that drive the creation and implementation of diversity practices. I explore the challenges and pressing issues that give shape to diversity behaviors and how they change over time. This book, then, provides a sociological interpretive account of how legal mandates, population demographics, global markets, corporate responsibility, and the critical mass of women and minorities affect the presence of diversity strategies.

Chapter Three

Corporations have neither bodies to be punished, nor souls to be condemned, they therefore do as they like.

—Edward Thurlow, 1st Baron Thurlow,
British Lawyer and Tory politician and
Lord Chancellor of Great Britain

Chapter Three
Hiring Problems or Hiring Myths?

I t is often argued by research scholars and practitioners that women and minorities have difficulty entering and advancing in the ranks of corporate America. Even after successful recruitment, it is no secret that corporate America is not a friendly environment for those who are not white males. Studies indicate that women and minorities are confronted with tokenism, lower pay, poor opportunities for career advancement and lack of mentoring, and often report feelings of isolation and exclusion in the firm. Women and minorities who do well in the corporation, at least in part, are considered as assimilating to company philosophy and culture. On the other hand, those who do not succeed are likely to be deemed as misfits.

Research on hiring women and minorities in the corporate sector has paid little attention to firm characteristics. In fact, when examining factors such as race and gender in work organizations, consideration is rarely given to differences in corporation size, type of industry, or geographical location. In this chapter, I examine the issues that pose barriers to hiring women and minorities. At the core of my analysis is the notion that firm characteristics and the presence of diversity strategies, together, influence the hiring of women and minorities. Variation in hiring difficulties of these groups experienced by certain types of corporations is considerable and reflects myriad controversial and relevant recruitment and hiring issues within the nation's information technology sector. Simply put, some corporations are just better than others in recruiting and hiring women and minority talent.

Hiring in the Information Technology (IT) Sector

Not all employment sectors face the same challenges or conditions when hiring underrepresented groups. For instance, banking, insurance, medicine, and law have their own character and milieu that shape their respective histories of attracting and hiring women and minorities. Most professions and occupations vary in their efforts, practices, policies, and structures in their employment of women and minorities. This is true for the information technology sector as well. According to recent employer surveys, issues related to the information technology workforce tend to center on several factors. Because of large numbers of job vacancies, high turnover, long time periods to fill positions, and relatively low unemployment rates, the information technology sector is experiencing substantive difficulty in hiring professionals, regardless of gender and racial or ethnic background (National Research Council 2001). However, when drawing attention to women and minorities especially, I am concerned with those organizational features and individual characteristics that impact a firm's decision to hire these groups. I focus attention on how certain information technology industries experience more or less difficulty in hiring women and minorities. I explore the conditions and qualifications for entry into the corporation and discuss how women and minorities respond to such conditions. In this chapter, I also offer an explanation of how diversity strategies serve as a means of coping with and addressing difficulties associated with hiring women and minorities.

"It is a serious crisis!" "The United States has an IT worker shortage!" "Help wanted: A call for action: America faces an IT labor shortage!" A wealth of news articles, business reports, federal statistics, and editorials proclaim the news that America was facing a severe shortage of workers in the information technology sector. Researchers and employer surveys sound the alarm that IT related job vacancies are outpacing the number of available skilled professionals. As perhaps one of the nation's most important sectors in the flattened global economy, it is no secret that for decades, the federal government has continued to put forth the claim

that there is a continuously inadequate supply of highly skilled and well-trained information technology scientists and engineers.

Millions and millions of federal grant dollars are allocated each year for developing individuals for careers in math- and science-related fields such as computer science and engineering. Special summer and enrichment programs, internships, fellowships, scholarships, and the like target women and minorities to develop their skills in information technology. Since the 1970s, the nation has identified the need for an increased number of scientists and engineers and, according to a vast number of federal reports, we continue to fall short of our goals to produce an *adequate* supply of them.

One might assume that major corporations would share the same sentiment as the federal government. Large corporations would indeed be seriously threatened by a labor shortage and its impact on their ability to remain competitive, innovative, and profitable. However, despite such claims and such arduous efforts to address the inadequate supply of scientists and engineers, my research suggests the opposite. Only 34 percent of corporations have difficulty in hiring information technology professionals. Two-thirds of corporations in this study who do not experience difficulty in hiring talent claim that a faltering economy, for the most part, has reduced the current demand for new hires and forced them to implement hiring practices that minimize labor costs. During her interview, Alisha, a human resources senior vice president, expressed this sentiment in the following way:

> You know, we really aren't faced with major hiring problems like we used to experience a few years ago … it's because of our freeze on hiring. The economy's slowdown and its effect on our customers has caused us to scale back on bringing in new hires. We just don't do the same amount of recruiting or anything … the company cannot afford to increase our labor costs, and instead we're now trying to reduce them. One way to do this is to use the talent we already have in the company.

Looking broadly across the information technology sector, attracting and hiring labor is not an issue—there appear to be no deficits. However, by industry type, difficulty in hiring professionals is concentrated in one specialty area of information technology—*the creation of software*. Sixty percent of software-intensive companies experience difficulty in hiring professionals, compared to only 23 percent of computer equipment development and testing laboratories and 25 percent of systems analyses and engineering companies. These companies are rarely impacted by changing labor needs and are typically accommodated by economic forces in the labor market. One interviewee, Bradley, a human resources senior manager, points out:

> There has been so much hype about a shortage of good talent in IT. This is not exactly true. You see, the IT industry is quite broad and diverse; it includes many areas of specialization, just like medicine, for example. My company produces hardware; you know, we build the machines, we create the hardware and so forth. We're the equipment gurus of IT. We don't have any problems finding workers but my colleagues over in the software world don't share our good fortune. We, on the other hand, always have large, qualified applicant pools.

As a general rule, computer software-intensive companies tend to attract and hire professionals with knowledge of general programming languages as well as experience working with industry-specific programming languages. Job positions that require software computer scientists and engineers also require specialized skill sets and training that usually are offered in four-year colleges and universities, while other IT industries only require a specific vocational certification. By default, this narrows the candidate pool immediately. Competing with popular college majors such as English, history, political science, biology, and business, computer science and engineering majors are few. For those students remotely interested in studying computer science, rumors of its association with "nerdy geeks" and being grounded in mathematics contribute to the low numbers of declared majors. In fact, many colleges and universities do not even offer majors related to computer science or computer engineering. Given these barriers to training, those pursuing and completing degrees in computer science and engineering constitute a relatively small prospective labor pool. Here is how one interviewee, Denise, a senior human resources manager, describes the situation:

> Although we might have 500 applicants for 25 positions, we might only find a couple of handfuls of folks that really meet our qualifications. We must be highly selective and choose the best and the brightest people ... Our firm really depends on it. We look for extraordinary skill sets ... very specialized skill sets among our applicants. See, software production requires that our scientists and engineers demonstrate the capacity to learn easily and quickly. They must be flexible, too. Our corporation recruits hard for our talent. We compete, most of the time, for new hires with other companies. You know, our reputation depends on getting and keeping the best talent out there.

The nation's cry of a worker shortage in information technology tends to refer to the *computer software industry*. Federal and business reports and journals of the trade usually fail to specify the type of information technology industry. This exaggerated contention that the United States is lagging in the world's most productive growth engine does not apply to the entire information technology sector. One industry does not reflect or represent the entire sector.

My research indicates that the computer software industry's difficulty in hiring individuals stems not from a faltering economy, but from the incredible effort to find highly qualified and well-trained professionals. The computer software industry's difficulty in hiring individuals stems not from a faltering economy, but from the incredible effort to find highly-qualified and well-trained professionals. This issue has been persistent and has nothing to do with hiring costs, freezes, or a reduction in human resources. The high selectivity of computer software professionals raises the issue of *who* is qualified and meets the conditions under which the corporation is seeking new talent. We will discuss this matter in more detail later in this chapter.

One might think that attracting and hiring new talent would not be a problem for Microsoft or IBM. These corporations are highly visible and high-ranking in their area of specialization and tend to have a longstanding favorable reputation among their employees. Young computer science and engineering graduates from competitive colleges and universities dream of working for large and competitive firms. Large and globally competitive corporations select, motivate, and guide students who are interested in joining their organizations. Their aggressive recruitment strategies include their presence at college job fairs and their affiliations and substantive ties with campus career services. Therefore it might be safe to assume that most large and highly visible corporations are successful at attracting and hiring new talent. This is not exactly the case. In fact, smaller companies are only *slightly* more likely to experience difficulty in hiring new talent compared to large corporations. Large and highly visible corporations, regardless of their recruitment efforts, face challenges when attempting to attract and hire new talent. The selection feature of hiring individuals may be impacted by a small selection pool, an inadequate selection pool, or perhaps both. Nonetheless, what is worth noting here is that large and desired employers are not invulnerable to hiring difficulties.

The preeminence of the great American corporation has been undermined not only by foreign competition but also by the entrepreneurial surge within the United States (Kanter 1977). This cannot apply more significantly to the high technology sector, which has presented a new and compelling alternative model of business success. Stories about overnight success resulting in billions of dollars are no longer unusual to hear in the boardroom. Small companies' success, primarily based on teamwork and innovation, has caused large corporations to adopt similar strategies and behaviors. The steady stream of change igniting in the 1980s and reaching its peak in the 1990s loosened structures and blurred boundaries in America's corporations. The information technology sector is a good example of this steady change and its impact on women and minorities.

The Supply of Women, Minority IT Talent

Over the past decade, the information technology sector has emerged as a leader on issues of workplace diversity. Consistent attention to diversity has been motivated by pressing industry concerns to remain globally competitive, innovative, and highly productive. In essence, during this period, the bottom line was the driving force for diversity and hence *required* the participation of individuals from its broadest possible talent pool. Corporations assert that attracting, developing, and retaining talent, *all* talent, are the key to sustaining and bolstering economic growth in the United States. In this view, diversity is a necessity and a benefit to the firm. However, I have found that efforts to create a more heterogeneous workplace are usually fraught with frustration and nuance.

Nearly 60 percent of corporations find it a daunting challenge to successfully recruit women and minorities. In fact, certain industries find it especially difficult. For example, computer equipment development firms, testing laboratories, and software development and programming companies experience the greatest difficulty in hiring women and minorities. These knowledge-intensive industries focus on research, testing, and software production. As such, they tend to impose more stringent hiring requirements controlled by an external environment, that is, formal education and professional training. By industry standards, these requirements are geared toward the exclusion of many women and minorities while, in turn, reflecting the traditional education and work experiences of males and non-minorities.

Not surprisingly, smaller corporations experience slightly more difficulty hiring women and minorities than do large ones. Given that large companies are typically more highly visible and generate higher revenue, chances are greatest that women and minorities are attracted and dedicated to firms where they can "retire well" and "be taken care of for life." Of equal importance is the "diversity seal of approval." Most women and minorities seek out the corporation that has earned the "Best Employer for Diversity Award." Translated, this means a better chance for career opportunities and advancement. These company behaviors are generally associated with large and older corporations.

Expectedly, some corporations, because of their geographic locale, experience greater difficulty in hiring women and minorities. The vast majority of corporations in the northeastern and western regions of the United States have trouble hiring women and minorities. Historically, these regions have occupied the lion's share of the information-technology labor force. However, most recent employment reports indicate that demand in the West for information technology professionals has steadily declined over the past decade, whereas there appears to be a resurgence of demand in the Northeast. Therefore, if demand is *low* in certain parts of the country, then it is evident that hiring, in general, would be minimal.

Prior to the 1980s, white males dominated their homogeneous careers as computer scientists and engineers. These professionals entered from preferred undergraduate programs at select colleges and universities as well as from specialized technical programs. These practices restricted women and minorities (with the exception of many Asians) who did not fit the white male model, often expressed as "one who fits the corporate culture." But the most commonly held belief concerning the low number of women and minorities is the notion that there exists a *small applicant pool*. It is the inadequate number of women and minority applicants that results in difficulty in hiring rather than the assumption that many women and minorities do not fit the corporate model. Instead, what is believed is that if more of them would apply, then more of them would be hired. During her interview, Alisha, a Human Resources Vice President located on the west coast, states:

> Well, it's difficult in a way that the [female and minority] pool is small. The candidate pool is very, very small and there are very many companies that are in competition to find the same skills of those individuals. That's what's so difficult—if there were a large pool it wouldn't be so difficult. As of now, we simply don't have enough of these individuals applying for jobs here. I think that there are not enough of them out there.

Understanding more fully the variation that exists among corporations that impacts the hiring of women and minorities, we can then choose more appropriate policies and programs to improve the quality of work life and promote equal employment opportunity. Understanding guides action. And action on women and minority issues may be critically important for the future of American society as a whole.

So far, this chapter has argued that women and minorities are in short supply. But in the IT sector, any warm body just won't do. Attention must be paid to the skill set and specialized ability of job candidates to do technical work. Prospective employees experience an arduous application process. It is difficult to get individuals to submit to it. Let me offer a short narrative from my study that highlights the criteria for selection from the perspective of a young, recent graduate who received a B.S. degree in computer systems engineering.

Marianna's resume was quite competitive. Having graduated from college only two years ago, she had already gained valuable work experience as a systems engineer at one of the nation's top software-development companies. She had decided that it was time to move to the big city. She wanted to relocate to a less remote area of the country. So, she submitted her resume to the nation's top-ranking software development company and was called in for an interview.

Four men—three Asian and one white—were responsible for screening Marianna's qualifications for the junior software engineer position. The interviewers made it clear that as a junior software engineer, Marianna would be responsible for assisting with, and even leading at times, the development of applications and Web services for the company's open billing platform. Currently, the division's platform consisted of seven Web services built on the WebLogic BEA platform and four services built on Tomcat with an Apache wrapper. Marianna's skills would be challenged by her ability to address shortcomings in existing technology and identify alternative forms in live production environments. Using technology such as SCRUM agile development models, developing and using testable codes, and being expected to come up with creative "out of the box" coding styles, Marianna's ability and willingness to be a team player would also be paramount. In addition, working with lead architects as well as other senior systems engineers was a requirement for this position.

Indeed, Marianna's employer of choice has no problem attracting job candidates. They are the best at what they do. However, it is unknown outside of the corporation how many inquiries culminate in completed applications. In other words, it is impossible to gauge just who is turned away from this company prior to completing their application and interview. Therefore, the company's ongoing claim that the qualified applicant pool is too small is questionable. The majority of technical job positions in Marianna's company require formal education, work experience, and ongoing training. It is rumored throughout this company that only two percent of those who inquire about positions are actually hired. Marianna was one of them.

As discussed in the scenario, research on and development of new technologies and products require a relatively high level of proficiency in technical knowledge and specialized skill sets *prior* to entry into the corporation. Some types of information technology work require individuals to demonstrate theoretical knowledge and well-developed reasoning, whereas other types require persons to visualize outcomes, anticipate problems, and manage projects, budgets, and people.

Formal Education and Training

In past years, different kinds of formal education have been required for different kinds of information technology work. For instance, research positions generally require post-baccalaureate degrees. Yet, the benefits of higher education in general (critical thinking, abstract reasoning skills) have enabled persons earning a baccalaureate degree in any discipline to be effective in many information technology intensive corporations.

Work involving installation, maintenance, repair, or modification of an IT artifact generally requires skills that are based on the specific characteristics of the particular software or hardware rather than on abstract concepts or theoretical knowledge. Hence, most times these types of positions require an associate's degree, vocational or technical training, or graduation from certificate programs and/or vendor certification. The information technology sector also makes jobs available to persons graduating from high school technical programs, although most graduates from these programs tend to pursue more technical training in community or technical colleges. Certainly, there is much variation in the types of education and training required for different types of information technology work (National Research Council 2001).

Seventy-five percent of corporations in the business of computer equipment development and testing laboratories *require* new hires to have at least a baccalaureate degree in an information technology related discipline. Nearly 70 percent of systems analyses and engineering corporations have similar requirements. However, this is not the case for the type of IT work involving installation, maintenance, repair, and

modifications. Less than half of these types of industries require a baccalaureate degree.

When introducing women and minorities into this discussion, many
of these hiring trends change. Regardless of the type of work, corporations tend to hire women and minorities with at least a bachelor's degree.
Corporations prefer to hire women and minorities who are college educated. In a word, the immediate requirement for employment for women
and minorities is *schooling*. That is the greatest inhibitor to entry into the
corporation for most women and minorities.

Informal Knowledge and Situated Learning

Alone, formal education and training do not make a competitive and
productive workforce. Although credentials from educational institutions
and training programs are highly attractive to most employers, recent
surveys indicate that *informal* knowledge and *situated* learning is essential
for effective job performance. Work styles and "situated" understandings
about materials, tools, and techniques are an integral part of a social
system at work, home, or school. In this view, informal knowledge and
situated learning, not derived from textbooks, work manuals, or company policies, are *contextualized*. In other words, skills learned or used in
one context, especially in certain information technology industries, are
not to be used in another. Thus, the notion that skills are *contextualized*
makes some employers reluctant to hire individuals based solely on their
academic performance in school or training programs.

Recall Marianna. Work experience was essential to her getting the
job interview. It is an intended part of the application selection process.
Unlike other professions where experience does not matter for entry, the
essence of technical work builds on a foundation of basic knowledge that
grows and is strengthened by more experience. Simply put, experience
translates into greater productivity across the corporation. Sandra, a
senior human resources manager, puts it this way in her interview:

> Our work here requires that our scientists and engineers are
> experienced *before* we offer them the job. We recruit people
> who not only know the technology but are familiar enough

to add to it—you know, advancing it. Most of the time, we need new hires to hit the ground running. There is no time for holding hands or walking folks through their work requirements. It's just like medicine. When the doctor shows up in the emergency room, you expect him to practice! Your health depends on it. As for the company, our production depends on it.

However, in other work environments, inexperience is actually desired. Some companies want employees with as close to blank slates as possible. Inexperience allows for the development and manipulation of work habits and attitudes. Again, this is not the preference of most industries in the information technology sector. In fact, labor studies conducted in this sector indicate that work experience—be it managerial or technical—is crucial for maintaining productivity in the corporation (Lee 1999; Salzman 2000).

More so than other industries, software development, programming, and systems analyses and engineering companies consider experience essential for entry into the corporation. This is no surprise. Also requiring at least a four-year degree in a related field, these industries do not offer on-the-job training. Rather, after hiring, they expect to build on individuals' existing technical knowledge to further the company's productivity and innovation. On-the-job training is considered too costly and time consuming. Large corporations provide CD-ROM versions of training that allow the individual employee to "self-train," as opposed to offering expensive classes or seminars.

Work Experience

In the case of recruiting women and minorities, regardless of type of industry, corporations prefer work experience. Work experience plus formal education and training are important conditions for hiring women and minorities. This suggests that the corporation seeks the *best of the best* highly qualified female and minority candidates, as most organizations compare minority applicants to their minority peers. They are expected to be "above" the average hire. This above-average expectation is one factor that may contribute to corporations' difficulties in hiring women and minority talent.

Nonetheless, one sure way of hiring women and minorities with formal education and work experience is to recruit them from other corporations. Evidence here indicates that this has become a popular hiring strategy among many companies. Information technology companies, especially those in the same industry type, are like close cousins. They are familiar with one another's innovations, productivity, and position in the marketplace. Likewise, they know of each others' employment trends. Should the proportion of women and minority professionals be as low as reported, then their extraordinary works and accomplishments in this sector are no secret. Their high visibility, resulting usually from their innovation, makes them well-known icons in their respective industries. As such, they are likely to be targets of competition among corporate peers and affiliated organizations. Higher salaries, stock options, advanced career opportunities, and other job attractions motivate them to leave one company for another. However, this "star swapping" fails to contribute to increasing the overall number of women and minorities in the industry. Instead, it allows for the corporation—those that can afford them—to benefit from the talents and specialized skills of a handful of females and minorities who have proven to be "above average" in the technology field. Such stardom often creates a work environment wherein "average" women and minorities find it difficult to enter and compete.

Given that corporations demonstrate a preference for hiring women and minorities with extraordinary skills and training, I do wonder, where does this leave females and minorities who are *not* the best of the best? Are they automatically excluded from entry into the firm? National data confirm again and again that these groups are underrepresented in college and university majors related to science and engineering. The lack of education and training are major barriers to entry into the corporation. Given that this sector is built on a highly skilled and educated workforce, the issue of hiring women and minority talent is directly tied to its primary suppliers—colleges and universities. However, if colleges and universities are not producing an adequate supply of women and minority talent, are corporations forced to hire *lesser* qualified women and minorities and develop them internally to demonstrate a commitment to workplace diversity? The answer is no.

One might expect that, in a highly technical work environment, the last thing to be encouraged would be a negotiation of individual characteristics—qualities of individuals such as level of ambition, assertiveness, and the right education and experience for the job. The precision of technical work allows little room for developing broad and general skills among new hires. Bringing in and dealing with the skills of lesser qualified individuals creates a wealth of problems. For example, special corporate programs purposed to develop the skill sets and provide important work experience for target groups, such as women and minorities, are commonly faced with claims of reverse discrimination and accusations of unfair favorable treatment. Threats of class action suits, discord in the workplace, and negative publicity contribute to a corporation's decision to be rigorous concerning individuals' job qualifications.

The Lesser Qualified

Historically, corporations may have been more lenient in working with inexperienced and lesser qualified, underrepresented groups. Nearly fifty years since the civil rights movement resulting in landmark passages of legislation ensuring equal employment opportunities, corporations have seen generations of women and minorities pass through their doors. No longer is there the same level of passion or unrelenting devotion to grow lesser qualified women and minorities into entry-level positions. A half century has brought with it some fundamental societal changes that have impacted the composition of the workplace in most American corporations. Women and minorities are earning competitive degrees and they have made inroads in work environments that were once exclusively male and non-minority.

Hiring lesser qualified individuals also contributes to a lag in production. Information technology industries are fast-paced. In order to remain competitive, corporations must develop and retain some of the most highly skilled and qualified scientists and engineers who are able to keep up with continuously changing technologies and innovation. Time spent training or preparing those individuals who are not up to speed with current applications, designs, troubleshooting, and "out-of-the-box" thinking translates into slower production. Although seen as an untapped talent pool, most corporations cannot afford to invest much time and many resources into lesser qualified women and minorities—the environment is simply too fast-paced and demanding.

Relatively few corporations in this study, less than 10 percent, actually hire less-qualified women and minorities. Industries relying on individuals with specialized skill sets do not lower their education and training requirements—even in the name of diversity. Most corporations interview women and minorities without the preferred credentials. However, they see great potential for future employment given additional formal education and work experience. This is true especially for the more knowledge-intensive industries. Unfortunately, this recognition of potential success in the corporation does not result in immediate hiring, nor is this often the case over time.

Recent employment surveys conducted in the information technology sector conclude that its future is contingent on behind-the-scenes technical gurus who orchestrate the interaction of numerous technologies to create comprehensive and, now more than ever, *secure* products. Credentials of recent hires who possess these specialized skill sets are formal education, resulting in an earned degree, specialized training, and information technology work experience. Corporations can ill afford to hire individuals who do not meet these qualifications.

During the past decade or so, when unable to find qualified job candidates, corporations typically turned to alternative strategies to meet their human resources needs. Outsourcing was one of the most popular ways of securing highly qualified employees. This turn toward employees outside the United States, particularly in India and South Asia, has been bedeviled with controversy.

Foreign Labor

Shifting jobs to low-wage countries, which is known as "offshore outsourcing," has created a political debate centering on issues such as unfair international trade and its devastating costs to U.S. workers. Outsourcing has been incredibly emotional given two dramatically different effects—it leads to layoffs and dislocation for thousands of U.S. workers, and can ultimately strengthen the U.S. economy. At the center of this outsourcing controversy has been the high-tech industry.

Critics of high-tech companies sound the alarm of exploitation when corporations sponsor foreign, skilled workers for green cards—a process that can take years. If these workers complain about any issue related to their employment, they can easily be deported. Most experts differ as to what is the greater worry—importing foreign workers or offshoring technology jobs to low-wage countries.

High-tech companies have not hesitated to relocate their call centers and even their software development jobs to places including India, the Czech Republic, and Russia because labor costs are lower and skilled workers abound. More recently, however, there is so much global demand for employees proficient in programming languages, engineering, and other skills requiring high-level technology knowledge that outsourcing cannot meet all U.S. needs. Interestingly, an overwhelming majority of corporations in this study (85 percent) report that they are not involved in outsourcing. Most corporations believe that it erects obstacles that are difficult to overcome. For smaller businesses, resources are not readily available to conduct outsourcing and language and cultural barriers pose challenges. As a result, many corporations are requiring that their professionals take on new and complex roles that involve additional tasks and interactions with colleagues outside the corporation.

At one point, outsourcing, especially in the context of hiring foreign workers, was seen as a threat to all American workers, but especially to women and minorities, who are the most difficult to recruit and often the least desirable candidates. Statistics often bear out the dismal picture of the proportions of women and minorities in the information-technology sector. Should these numbers prove true, then, the presence of foreign workers, operating under temporary visas, creates a force of competition that is nearly impossible to reckon with. However, in the midst of upheavals about outsourcing and its affects, many corporations were determined to leave no stone unturned. They adopted and implemented *diversity strategies* geared to attract, hire, and retain U.S.-born women and minorities.

Understanding that women and minorities face substantive barriers to entry into the information-technology labor force, diversity strategies are a route to acquiring entry. However, corporations that manage key diversity initiatives are *not* exempt from difficulties associated with hiring women and minorities. In fact, over 60 percent of corporations experience difficulty hiring women and minorities despite their adoption of diversity strategies. In some cases, then, the existence of diversity strategies may reflect the severity of and response to difficulty in hiring women and minority talent. There are certain industries that tend to adopt diversity strategies. An overwhelming 80 percent of software intensive corporations do so. On the other hand, only 37 percent of non-software and research intensive companies have strategies focused on diversity.

The adoptions of diversity strategies, in large part, are a function of corporations' efforts to reduce difficulty in hiring women and minorities. Corporations with diversity strategies have a *higher* proportion of women and minorities compared to those without them. This suggests that diversity strategies are related to the retention of women and minorities as well. In the case of Asian Americans, the presence of diversity strategies does not matter. The proportion of Asian Americans is about the same in corporations with and without diversity strategies. Historically, Asian Americans have maintained a higher representation than other minority groups in certain information technology industries. Recently, they have even surpassed the numbers of white males in high-tech companies. Rebecca, a vice president for human resources in this study, states:

> Diversity strategies do make a difference. I have experienced that without them, our numbers of women and minorities have been lower. The strategies allow everyone to understand that the company is serious about bringing in women and minorities. And we are accountable to this. It kind of pulls everyone along ... you know, we're all on the same page ... at least in terms of company goals. Our diversity plans have truly made a difference. We have at least 15 to 20 percent more women and minorities on board because of our long-term plans to diversify our work environments.

To summarize, a careful look at corporations' perceptions of difficulty in hiring talent shows that what appeared to be a supply problem may really be a demand issue. Most corporations do not experience great difficulty finding new hires. But, when looking for women and minorities, the vast majority of corporations are challenged. Women and minority hiring challenges are driven by the applicant pool, which is not fixed or predictable. Rather, it is contingent on the preparation that comes from outside the corporation—at the college or university level. The challenge of hiring women and minorities also varies by the nature of work. More so than other industries, software and research- and knowledge-intensive companies require new hires to have earned college credentials. Industries involving more practical skills—maintenance, repair, and installation—are less likely to require formal education and specialized knowledge.

However, it is important to understand that regardless of industry type, in the case of women and minority applicants, formal education and specialized knowledge is preferred and expected. Another avenue for hiring women and minorities that is sought by corporations is work experience. Despite the nature of technical work, corporations highly value work experience. Given its proven significant effect on productivity, experience ensures employers that new hires can quickly, easily, and effectively meet industry demands.

It is certainly no secret that women and minorities are at the lower tiers of earning college degrees in IT related disciplines. Without technical credentials, most women and minorities will find themselves knocking on the door without gaining entry. Corporations do not hire marginally qualified women and minorities. Although applicants show much potential, corporations do not hire and develop this potential internally. On the other hand, corporations do develop strategies to accomplish their work. They revert to outsourcing and hire foreign workers. In the case of women and minorities, corporations create and implement diversity strategies to avert barriers to entry and acquire untapped talent.

Although these issues are critical for understanding an important dimension of the hiring challenges and conditions faced by corporations, what is of primary interest here is why and how the corporation responds to them. It is my contention that diversity strategies are outcomes of not only corporate business goals but also other social forces that guide and influence their decision to implement diversity structures and behaviors. The succeeding chapters offer analyses and discussions of how these social forces shape how corporations address diversity.

Chapter Four

No business is above Government; and Government must be empowered to deal adequately with any business that tries to rise above Government.

—Franklin Delano Roosevelt,
32nd President of the United States

Chapter Four
Legal Mandates and Political Choices

O ne of the keys to understanding what drives a corporation to adopt and implement diversity strategies to examine the relationship between perceptions of legal mandates and political choices and the presence of diversity strategies. Often, corporations attempting to implement diversity structures and behaviors find it difficult to consistently focus attention on diversity given the winds of the economy, politics, and legal actions. Nonetheless, the substance of diversity behaviors originates from the legal and political environment. Hence, assumptions about their influence and contribution to corporations' decisions to adopt diversity strategies should be examined closely.

Institutional Environments

Early ideas about the influence of the external environment on organizations began with the assumption that organizations do not exist freely. Rather, they must behave in accordance with the laws and traditions of their societies. That is, organizations are forced to adapt to the state and dominant subcultures. This institutional perspective rests on the notion that organizations must act in accordance with the rules, laws, and the traditions of their societies. Put simply, the power of the state permeates the boundaries of the organization and impacts its decisions and behaviors accordingly.

Classic studies on organizations and their environments by Meyer and Rowen (1977) and DiMaggio and Powell (1983) argue that the state exerts "coercive" pressure on organizations to adapt their structures to institutionalized norms. More recent research maintains that the American state has a powerful influence on employment relations policies within work organizations (Collins 1989; Baron, Dobbins, and Jennings 1996). In fact, legal mandates regulating employment practices result in ambiguous principles that provide organizations latitude to construct their own meaning of compliance in ways that meet both external demands and managerial interests (Edelman 1992).

This institutional logic permeates the corporate world. The federal government's role in reducing employment discrimination continues to be significant. Many corporations perceive Equal Employment Opportunity and Affirmative Action mandates to be critical in the recruitment and hiring of women and minorities. However, as a motivation for adopting *diversity strategies*, many corporations fail to attest to the importance of nondiscrimination employment laws. Arguably, as an intervention, federal policies *alone* are important in driving the corporation to pursue women and minorities. The *law* continues to carry much weight in influencing corporations' hiring decisions. Several corporations perceive diversity strategies as loosely tied to laws, yet they contend that they are a prevailing motivation for corporations' interest in recruiting and hiring women and minorities.

Certainly, the idea of valuing and doing diversity in American corporations is commonplace. In fact, diversity, for many businesses, has become an important business strategy. Nevertheless, it is the longstanding historical role of federal mandates that continues to *regulate* corporate hiring structures and behaviors toward women and minorities. This leaves us with a critical question about the relationship between laws such as Equal Employment Opportunity and Affirmative Action and corporate diversity strategies: Is "doing diversity" the same as complying with Equal Employment Opportunity guidelines and implementing Affirmative Action programs? The interpretation rather than the letter of the law comes into focus when examining this relationship.

Diversity Strategies *and* Affirmative Action?

As diversity interventions moved into place several years ago, influential groups such as academicians, the media, and national and political organizations argued that workplace diversity initiatives would soften, dilute, and lessen the original tenets of Affirmative Action. Some national and political organizations even claimed that corporate diversity was designed to ensure that women and minorities experienced *greater* difficulty earning promotions and advancements in the corporation. While this argument seems counterintuitive at first glance, it is important to realize that these strategies are not federally mandated, regulated, or standardized. They exist at the whim of the firm and can be easily manipulated, giving corporations the ability to present the outward appearance of diverse hiring, without actually changing their hiring practices with respect to women and minorities at all. Moreover, critics interpreted corporate diversity as nonsubstantive and mere symbolic gestures of acting affirmatively. On the other hand, many scholars and professional organizations asserted that diversity strategies strengthen Equal Employment Opportunity and Affirmative Action by underscoring and building on its foundational principles and guidelines. In fact, diversity behaviors are viewed as broadening the original tenets of civil rights legislative programs and their applicability to the workplace. Like these critics, senior managers in this study have their own perceptions about the invisible chain that binds together Equal Employment Opportunity guidelines, Affirmative Action programs, and corporate diversity initiatives.

For many corporations, the relationship between Equal Employment Opportunity and Affirmative Action is clear—there really isn't one. Equal Employment Opportunity and Affirmative Action do not mandate formal strategies focused on hiring women and minorities. The longstanding role of government as a key player in ensuring equal employment opportunities has now shifted to a shared responsibility with the corporation itself. Laws alone are no longer the primary motivator for recruiting and hiring women and minorities. According to one interviewee, Shelia, a senior vice president for corporate diversity, diversity efforts, as opposed to Equal Employment Opportunity and Affirmative Action mandates, are driven by organizational goals, not mandates:

> Our diversity efforts are *not* related to Affirmative Action or Equal Employment Opportunity mandates. We are not *required* to develop and implement diversity practices. Diversity goes beyond policies like Affirmative Action. It is time for us to go beyond […] to move forward […] we must move forward to remain competitive. When you ask corporations are they doing diversity because the courts say you have to, the answer is no.

Expanding beyond the legal requirements and expectations of Equal Employment Opportunity and Affirmative Action, diversity strategies position the corporation to meet corporate goals that represent the interests and decisions of management. In this regard, diversity strategies do not stand alone, nor do they apply to only one area of the corporation. These strategies are fused with important goals throughout the corporation and in accordance with its vision and mission.

In particular, the notion of Equal Employment Opportunity and Affirmation Action as a "starting point" to provide equal opportunities for women and minorities is shared by many corporations. No matter what policies or programs the government opposes or legislates, corporations assert that there is a sense of a "moral contract" with society to provide equal employment, opportunities, and financial reward. Pushing the Affirmative Action envelope, corporations desire to move to a broader concept—managing diversity. Diversity of all sorts—gender, race, culture, and age—aids corporations in their pursuit of excellence, which relies on a broad range of diverse populations.

While a variety of employment practices exist within the corporation, diversity initiatives, unlike legal mandates, are not shared or accounted for by entities *outside* the organization. Instead, several human resources professionals report that diversity is a creation of the corporation itself. Hence, the adoption of diversity strategies can be conceptualized as strategic responses to meeting industry needs, whatever they are. One human resources vice president, Yvonne, put it this way in her interview:

> Diversity is far beyond and far more reaching than Affirmative Action requirements. You can do Affirmative Action and

never, ever get anywhere near the things that people are doing in the area of diversity, because Affirmative Action is just the minimum and expected. So one is driven by law and minimum requirements, and the other one [diversity] is driven by the aspect of the company, the right thing to do [...] strategic concerns and initiatives [...] doing business, becoming the employer of choice [...] to be able to hire, especially if you're a specialty company needing a lot of different intellectual needs, like ours.

Physical Space and Structures

One critical component in establishing a distinction between the functions of Equal Employment Opportunity, Affirmative Action and diversity is the structural composition of office space, managerial positions, and reporting lines. For a number of corporations, preceding the adoption of diversity strategies, changes were typically instituted in the composition of human resources management departments. In most cases, these departments are considered home for most managers responsible for carrying out diversity plans. Changes occur through the process and outcome of establishing independent roles and job functions. For example, some corporations seek to establish legitimacy when adopting diversity strategies. In doing so, corporations choose to create a managerial position responsible for implementing diversity strategies exclusively. An individual and/or staff are appointed to manage and provide oversight for the corporations' hiring and retention activities based on its specific diversity goals. Separately, the corporation houses an Affirmative Action officer who is responsible for aiding the corporation in its commitment to equal employment opportunity and ensuring nondiscrimination throughout the workplace as established by the federal government.

Although some job functions and responsibilities may overlap, separate structures (i.e., office spaces, reporting lines, and managerial positions) address any confusion resulting from those job activities that straddle the boundaries of other departments or units. These structural changes attempt to make clear the distinction between Equal Employment Opportunity, Affirmative Action, and diversity. Yvonne recalls:

> When we first adopted diversity, Diversity and EO/AA were actually together, reporting to the same person, but the diversity person and I, together, agreed that it would be better if we were separated. And we were separated because we ourselves felt that people in the corporation weren't understanding the difference between EO/AA and diversity, so we asked to be separated so that people would begin to understand the difference between the two. Now, almost ten years later, we [the EEO/AA officer and the Diversity officer] report to the same person—the head of Corporate Diversity.

Diversity Strategies and Government Policy

However, not every corporation shares the same view on the relationship between Equal Employment Opportunity and diversity. Several corporations attest that the key to understanding corporate diversity is government policy. They believe that government policy inspires corporations to adopt diversity strategies. Historically, diversity efforts in corporate America emerged in *response* to the declining approval of Affirmative Action programs. As evidenced here, 85 percent of corporations adopted diversity strategies in the early 1990s—the hallmark of the backlash on Affirmative Action programs.

For over half a century, many corporations have benefited from Affirmative Action programs as they help accomplish important organization goals. Many corporations perceive Affirmative Action practices as creating opportunity and helping to eliminate both conscious and inadvertent discrimination by developing and using the full potential of the entire society. This is not only critical for the nation's economic growth but also for our social well-being and responsibilities as global leaders. Furthermore, several corporations believe that the absence of Affirmative Action practices raises concern that, despite big gains in the 1960s in certain industries, the elimination of preferences would result in a certain amount of backsliding even if largely unintentional.

Other corporations contend that as long as nondiscrimination laws remain on the books—and they will—a national means of implementing them is needed. Affirmative Action practices are favored over the alternative—an uncertain environment where the absence of clear guidelines would expand the potential for vulnerability to legal sanctions or, perhaps even worse, chaos in the corporation. And, diversity strategies are *dependent* upon this knowledge.

Many corporations consider Affirmative Action practices to be good business practices. As such, they refer to competitive advantage, global competition, and the global economy. Affirmative Action programs spark a level of creative energy that results in imagination, which leads to a successful company over time. This is essential to companies in the business of producing information technology. What a great foundation from which diversity strategies can build.

As many corporations see it, Equal Employment Opportunity, Affirmative Action, and diversity initiatives are inextricably linked. The federal policies are required *complements* to diversity. Diversity would not be possible *without* the compliance effect of Equal Employment Opportunity and Affirmative Action, because these plans are indeed comparable to most diversity strategies. That is, Equal Employment Opportunity and Affirmative Action plans are concerned with proportional racial and gender imbalances in the workplace, and diversity initiatives are designed to create and maintain a diverse work environment. Thus, these mandates shape diversity behaviors in such a way that they confirm each others' goals and outcomes. From this perspective, they are interdependent. During his interview, Walter, a senior manager of corporate diversity, states:

> There is a strong relationship between Affirmative Action and diversity. Companies that say there's no relationship [...] I mean, we [diversity professionals] focus on representation; Affirmative Action focuses on representation. We work on employee relations, which has the Affirmative Action piece tied closely to them, and their tracking numbers—number of hires, representation, equal employment opportunity—which is all to me a part of diversity. Diversity is more focused on inclusion

where Affirmative Action is more about women and minorities. But this is a big piece of our diversity strategy, improving
the representation of women and minorities. So, saying they
don't relate to each other—I disagree.

Interestingly, less than 10 percent of corporations claim that there is no
need for "strategic" efforts focused on hiring women and minorities. In
fact, these views are rare. For this handful of corporations, diversity is not
an issue. Established within the past twenty years or so, these companies
maintain that their burgeoning industries are not faced with or challenged
by issues associated with hiring women and minorities. They assert that
they have "evolved" beyond the possibility of such issues. In fact, they
have really never had to deal with them. These corporations argue that
they are "global" and, as such, represent a nondiscriminatory *environment*. This opens up a new dimension for thinking about racial and gender diversity. The global view is tied to a global community comprising
racial, ethnic, and culturally diverse groups, which ultimately translates
into one thing—growing viable billion-dollar markets. However, I am
not convinced that this explanation holds true. The global status of a
corporation does not mean that it has evaded the longstanding issues
of hiring decisions concerning women and minorities, but it does suggest one thing—perhaps these corporations use their global status as a
justification for ignoring them completely.

Compliance

Adhering to federal guidelines and compliance concerning equal employment and nondiscrimination is viewed as simply obeying the law.
Otherwise, developing and implementing diversity activities in line with
or beyond federal policies is not the best use of time for the corporation.
In fact, these efforts are perceived as passé and limiting. As one senior
manager put it, "We don't discriminate; we can't afford to. We hire the
best and the brightest and they include people from a broad spectrum of
life. We are beyond discrimination; we are a global company."

It appears as if the most effective means of getting corporations to
pay attention to racial and gender discrimination is to file a lawsuit. The

landmark case against American Telephone and Telegraph (AT&T) in 1972 set the stage for future court cases concerning employees' claims of discrimination. Decided almost forty years ago, AT&T agreed to pay a hefty $38 million to employees discriminated against by the corporation.

WalMart, the nation's largest retailer, is a prime example of the reality of legal sanctions and public scrutiny. Over the past few years, insidious bias and prejudice characterized their hiring practices, giving rise to numerous lawsuits by aggrieved employees. Similarly, the world's leading technology corporation, Microsoft, was hit with one of the largest discrimination suits, which was filed by seven African American employees—$5 billion in damages was awarded to the plaintiffs. The automobile industry is not excluded. Nine white-collar workers at Ford Motor Company filed a multimillion dollar class-action age-discrimination suit, making it the first legal challenge to the company's controversial employee evaluation process.

Texaco's agreement to pay $140 million to employees who accused the company of racial discrimination in its promotion process came after three other major discrimination cases against State Farm, Shoney's Incorporated, and Lucky Stores, in which payment to resolve federal suits charging discrimination exceeded $100 million. Home Depot, Publix Super Markets, Motel 6, Dun & Bradstreet, Smith Barney, and Coca-Cola are also among hundreds of large corporations facing significant discrimination suits. The past three decades have seen a constant, fierce debate over how well corporations have rid themselves of discrimination. Women and racial minorities have more than tripled their presence in corporate management jobs since the 1970s, according to government reports. But members of these groups continue to complain of discrimination. One change is apparent, however. Complaints have shifted from those concerning hiring biases to harassment and discrimination in pay and promotion.

The overwhelming majority of corporations, 98 percent, claim that lawsuits are a primary factor affecting the decision to adopt and implement diversity strategies. Kevin, a senior HR director, states, "The firm cannot afford these lawsuits. These days, they are very costly, both financially and in terms of the company's public image. So, we use our diversity initiatives to protect us from possible legal action." On the contrary, some corporations assert that large discrimination settlements have little effect on their bottom line but a considerable impact on their public image and reputation. From the court of law to the court of public opinion lie criticism and negative press.

Allegations of discrimination in major U.S. corporations bring about unfavorable attention from highly visible, national organizations. Let's look at the role of the NAACP. In 2008, WalMart received a C+ grade, which was the top grade awarded in the merchandising category—the average grade was a C. The Economic Reciprocity Initiative (ERI) grades major corporations on their business practices with respect to African Americans. This evaluation is a viable means for the NAACP to measure efforts or the lack thereof in important areas such as hiring, promotion, procurement, philanthropy, and marketing. Several corporations in the study, including Nordstrom Inc. and Sears, Roebuck and Company received failing marks for lack of participation. Others seemed to court the NAACP, including WalMart, which donated $500,000 to the organization. Negative views associated with discrimination affects the corporation's attractiveness to women and minorities as well as potential minority business partners.

It is inevitable that discrimination lawsuits, however, impact employment policies—for the better. Corporations are likely to implement change resulting from legal sanctions, settlements, or public scrutiny in order to reduce their risk of future vulnerability to legal action. A vast majority of corporations report that it is legal action, primarily, that precipitated the implementation of their diversity initiatives. However, compared to the courts, less of a factor is the federal Equal Employment Opportunity Commission (EEOC).

The EEOC provides the force behind Title VII of the 1964 Civil Rights Act. This federal provision seeks to eradicate discrimination in employment in the United States. Administratively, the EEOC requires private firms to report the numerical distribution of minority workers. Over the past forty years, under the direction of the U.S. Congress, the EEOC has initiated civil suits in district courts in response to alleged discrimination and discriminatory patterns and practices against limited numbers of large employers (Purcell 1977). In 1973, the EEOC gained legitimacy and recognition by winning a consent decree from the landmark AT&T case. At the time, the EEOC created a system that tracked discriminatory practices in corporate America and received a significant amount of funding to hire more investigators and attorneys.

This demonstration of enforcement was a major impetus for corporations to revisit and bolster their hiring and promotion practices for minorities. A few years later, the EEOC would bring suits against some of the nations' most powerful corporations including Exxon, General Motors, Sears, Texaco, and Coca-Cola. Many corporations would end their struggle with the EEOC as signatories to binding consent decrees, obligating themselves to change their employment practices. By the mid 1970s, every large corporation in the United States had on board an EEO compliance officer and, in some cases, these individuals were given broad authority for hiring and promoting minorities (Thomas 1999). The process of investigating the validity of discrimination claims brings with it the tendency to smear publicly the image of the corporation while igniting the power of marginalized employees.

On average, 82,000 complaints are filed each year with the EEOC. Of these complaints, charges of discrimination based on race and gender far outnumber those based on age, national origin, religion, or disability (Equal Employment Opportunity Commission 2006). However, many civil rights experts agree that while the EEOC has concentrated its attention and resources on some of the most promising cases, it has also created a bottleneck or become a dead end for many others. The EEOC's heightened politicalization over the years is demonstrated by its presidential appointments, backlog of thousands of cases, and inadequate funding. People seeking assistance from this federal agency may be dissuaded from pursuing action. But by law, employees must complain to the EEOC before filing a discrimination suit in federal court.

Nonetheless, the legal enforcement of equal employment opportunity within and outside the courts has required corporate practices to be responsive to the employment conditions of women and minorities. Whether it is the costly impact of lawsuits or the unfavorable attention that they bring, many human resources professionals interviewed noted that corporations' behaviors are shaped by legal actions. For example, one interviewee, Sandra, a vice president for corporate diversity, puts it this way:

Let's look at discrimination lawsuits, for example, the lawsuit that Texaco was charged with or the lawsuit that Coca-Cola was charged with. When an organization is defending itself in a court of law against a suit where they've been sued for some discriminatory practice, a lot of information gets dragged into those lawsuits. So to the extent that a corporation can point to a lot of what we would call "diversity activities," say a minority leadership program or an aggressive program for recruiting women into nontraditional female roles, or other things that you might think of as not primarily for the purpose of complying with the law, but for the purpose of enhancing the value of diversity for the corporation [...] to the extent that the corporation can point to diversity activities, it can improve its chances overall of doing well in the lawsuit.

However, this is not all. The impact of recent lawsuits on major corporations, in general, has captured the attention of important politicians and public policy. The White House and U.S. Senate have distinguished their interest in corporations' battles with class action lawsuits in particular. When viewed in this way, legislative efforts such as tort reform exist to curb corporations' accountability for unlawful behaviors such as civil rights violations. In fact, many legal experts argue that tort reform efforts are really about taking away people's rights to go to court and taking away access to courts, thereby undermining their constitutional right to trial by jury.

In February 2005, in a State of the Union address, President Bush urged lawmakers to rewrite tort law to do away with class action lawsuits that, he suggested, have become a drag on the United States economy. The president won an initial victory in tort reform when a bill sought by corporations to curb class action lawsuits advanced in the Senate. This legislation transfers most class action lawsuits from state courts to more stringent federal courts and is the first in a package of changes to the tort system sought by the Bush administration. In the State of the Union address, President Bush offered these words:

To make our economy stronger and more competitive, Americans must reward, not punish, the efforts and dreams of entrepreneurs. Small business is the path of advancement, especially for women and minorities. So we must free small businesses from needless regulation and protect honest job creators from junk lawsuits. Justice is distorted and our economy is held back by irresponsible class actions and frivolous claims—and I urge Congress to pass legal reforms this year.

Federal Contracts

Other governmental influence on the adoption of diversity strategies is exercised by participation in federal contracts. Forty-two percent of corporations identify federal contracts as a motivator for adopting diversity strategies. Those with federal contracts or subcontracts of $50,000 or more are required to comply with federal hiring guidelines or else have federal funding withdrawn. Data collected by Heckman and Payner (1989) indicate that a greater number of government contracts are awarded to companies with fewer incidents of alleged discrimination. Also, these authors found that federal contract-compliance programs significantly improve employment opportunities for minorities.

Over 70 percent of corporations who adopt diversity strategies participate in federal contracts. By default, federal contract compliance programs motivate the adoption of diversity strategies. For many corporations, the threat of losing great sums of federal dollars propels them to manage and maintain strategies focused on women and minorities. According to one interviewee, Kevin, there is an important relationship between federal contracts and diversity activities:

> If you're a firm of this size and you do business with the federal government, you have to comply. [...] I mean, theoretically, diversity helps you in your marketing to diverse populations for employment opportunities with the organization. Yes, diversity plans help with compliance. If we're not in compliance, then we lose lots of money and the company is not going

to stand for that. So, we do all that we can to not lose our funding.

Foreign Labor Laws

Despite the heavy load of federal mandates involving allegations of discrimination often followed by arduous lawsuits, corporations also find themselves adjusting to political environments that entail international labor issues—for example, the foreign-born worker and the H-1B visa program. Much research shows that there is a continued heavy reliance on H-1B visa programs by employers in certain sectors, especially in information technology, but also in higher education, teaching, nursing, and other professional jobs. The information technology industries are global and are growing steadily in this direction. Countries other than the United States supply and produce information technology products, services, and talent. Hence, the role of foreign workers in information technology is salient and requires attention. The employment of foreign individuals in the United States workforce is quite controversial and continues to be the subject of a national political debate. Concerning information technology, foreign workers have, in essence, passed the relevance test (Kanter 1978). On the whole, they have proven to be positive contributors to the United States economy.

There are several "attractions" in employing foreign workers in the United States IT sector. First, foreign workers demonstrate specialized knowledge in software engineering and they tend to possess advanced degrees in information technology related disciplines as well as professional training prior to arriving in the country. When corporations are faced with inadequate applicant pools, they may well turn to foreign talent given their specialized knowledge and training. Second, most foreign workers are facilitators of connections between their country of origin and the United States. Third, rarely dismissed is the argument that information technology corporations are able to reduce labor costs associated with foreign workers. This claim rests on the empirical findings that foreign individuals are willing to work for less pay than comparably trained U.S. workers.

These popular justifications for hiring foreign workers were sold to Congress and the public in order to alleviate significant "shortages" of workers in certain and necessary industries. However, the story here is a bit more complicated. Ideally, H-1B visas were granted to corporations to access foreign workers on a temporary basis to supplement the U.S. workforce and to provide a means for companies to attract uniquely skilled and qualified workers. The H-1B visa was good for a period of up to three years with the possibility of a renewal of a second three-year period.

As to the issue of job vacancies and qualifications—the law does not require corporations to demonstrate that there is a shortage of U.S. workers for a particular job or that they have tried and failed to find qualified U.S. workers. In fact, according to the Center for Immigration Studies, many job openings are never advertised or offered to U.S. workers. Even more startling, as documented by the advocacy group Bright Future Jobs, some corporations are openly conducting "H-1B Visa Only" recruiting campaigns—literally advertising that U.S. citizens and legal immigrants need *not* apply. The U.S. Labor Department maintains that this practice is legal.

Most industry reports indicate that H-1B workers must have and must fill a job that requires at least a bachelor's degree or equivalent experience. However, prospective workers need not demonstrate any special expertise or fill any extraordinary need. In fact, more than half of the jobs filled by H-1B workers in 2005 were classified as "entry-level" or "trainee" by the employer on the application. Most H-1B workers are relatively young. Because 65 percent of H-1B workers are twenty-four to thirty-four years of age, few of them can realistically be considered to have demonstrated exceptional accomplishment. Forty-five percent have no more than a bachelor's degree, while only five percent have a doctorate.

As to the issue of salaries and compensation, the law does require that corporations pay H-1B workers what is known as the "prevailing wage"—a salary that is comparable to what a U.S. worker earns. This provision is intended to discourage corporations from hiring foreign workers at lower salaries. Yet, these regulations have proven ineffective. According to the U.S. Department of Labor, corporations pay H-1B workers an average of $16,000 dollars less per year than U.S. workers in the same job and location (Center for Immigration Studies, *Low Salaries for Low Skills: Wages and Skill Levels for H-1B Computer Workers*, 2005). Specifically, the median salary offered to H-1B workers is $60,000 per year (Department of Homeland Security *Characteristics of Specialty Occupation Workers H-1B* 2008).

Corporations need only indicate on the applicant's employment documentation that they will pay a prevailing wage and that the workers they are sponsoring are not laid-off U.S. workers. There is no authority that checks these claims. The U.S. Department of Labor has no authority to investigate applications unless they receive a complaint from an employee. Therefore, there is no governing authority that checks to see if the business really exists, if there is an actual job opening, or if the salary offered is really paid. The process is automated; as long as the employer signs the form and includes a check, the application is approved (Center for Immigration Studies 2005).

Despite the relative advantages to hiring foreign workers, there are serious negative impacts as well. The crux of the debate concerning foreign information technology workers is that the use of foreign workers has deleterious effects on U.S. workers. Critics contend that the increase in the supply of foreign information technology workers detrimentally affects U.S. workers by job displacement and the suppression of wages. It stands to reason that individuals most vulnerable to the arrival and employment of foreign information technology workers are women and minorities.

Central to the issues described here is the way in which foreign information technology workers enter the U.S. labor force. Direct recruitment from abroad and change or adjustments in the status of an individual residing in the U.S. are major ways for obtaining U.S. employment. Direct recruitment typically refers to sponsorship from a U.S. firm or its affiliates. This is the usual means by which most foreign individuals enter the information technology workforce, although for a limited period of time, the U.S. requires foreign individuals to possess temporary visas in order to enter the workforce. But most relevant to information technology industries is the H-1B visa made available to foreign workers for no more than six years in a "specialty occupation." Work areas in the specialty occupation category include computer programming and engineering.

It is no secret that the H-1B visa is favored among information technology corporations. According to the U.S. Immigration and Naturalization Service, nearly 60 percent of all H-1B visa holders are employed by IT intensive companies. Similarly, according to the U.S. Citizenship and Immigration Service, computer-related occupations are by far the most popular among H-1B visa holders, making up 42 percent of total petitions. Not surprisingly, the information technology sector has called for increasing or eliminating the H-1B visa cap. Although the U.S. government's fiscal year 2011 has set the H-1B visa cap at $65,000, the comprehensive immigration bill recently passed in the Senate would raise the yearly limit to $115,000. However, during the 1990s, before the terrorist attacks in 2001, the H-1B visa cap was as high as $195,000. Congress began reducing the number because of concerns about national security and pressure from trade protectionists who believed that information technology jobs should be available to American workers exclusively.

Motivated by the idea that there are simply not enough qualified and skilled Americans to fill vacant positions, the proposed increase in the H-1B visa cap is intended to help bridge the alleged vacancy gap. According to the U.S. Bureau of Citizenship and Immigration Services, this is the third consecutive year and the eighth time in the last ten years that the allotment of H-1B visas has reached the determined limit prior to the beginning of the federal fiscal year.

Critics of the H-1B visa program contend that information technology corporations are not drawn to foreign workers because of labor shortages but rather because of financial incentives. Research shows that information technology corporations hire H-1B workers in jobs requiring lower skill levels thus resulting in lower wages, less senior job titles, smaller signing bonuses, lower pay, and less compensation over time (Salzman 2000). Federal immigration data indicate that wages for 85 percent of foreign computer programmers hired under the H-1B visa program earned less than the median U.S. wage for the same occupations.

In this view, critics are concerned with the impact of the H-1B visa program on wages and benefits for domestic workers. Such financial incentives could extend to the lower wages and poorer benefits for U.S.

workers. Most critics of the H-1B visa program focus attention on the permanence of foreign information technology workers in the U.S. labor force. In other words, will the increased supply of foreign labor under the H-1B visa program inevitably decrease the demand for U.S. workers?

The foreign and H-1B visa phenomenon is of great concern to those troubled by the underrepresentation of women and minorities in the information technology sector. My study found that nearly 90 percent of corporations who adopt diversity strategies perceive that the H-1B visa program is a force to be reckoned with. Some researchers argue that the declining number of women and the scant percentage of minorities in information technology are linked to the H-1B visa program. As for women in the information technology labor force, their under-representation is related to the disproportionate number of male H-1B visa holders. Federal data indicate that women make up less than 25 percent of temporary workers and trainees admitted to the U.S. under the H-1B visa program.

U.S. racial minorities are also impacted by the H-1B visa program. Given the existence of employment discrimination, the H-1B visa program is believed to *discourage* corporations from recruiting and hiring women and minorities. A study commissioned by the Coalition for Fair Employment in Silicon Valley (no longer in business), a group claiming to represent thousands of minority professionals, found that out of eighty-five information technology corporations, thirteen actively discriminated against women and minorities, and twenty-four lacked minority recruitment plans required under the guidelines of their federal contracts.

In fact, one company in the Coalition's study was ordered to pay nearly $215,000 in back pay and other civil remedies for improperly denying low-level technical jobs to Latino applicants, whom the Department of Labor determined were qualified for the positions. In the face of such discriminatory hiring practices, the H-1B visa program serves as a "legitimate" route for information technology corporations to disregard U.S.-born women and minority talent. For instance, one interviewee, William, a senior manager of the office of diversity, states:

The H-1B visas are controversial, especially when we are faced with issues of hiring racial minorities in the U.S. There is no way that we can lose when hiring foreign workers who are already technically trained in the areas we need them. I feel bad about the issue [...] but what has happened is that we've found a "better" source of labor and it works for us right now. I do agree that it makes it more difficult for us to hire minorities, especially when they lack the skills or education we want. This is why they must try to stay competitive ... we're now a global society. No longer are we limited to our borders. And the company is going to do whatever it needs to in order to remain competitive. There's simply too much competition out here these days. And honestly, sometimes hiring someone from India or China is best for the corporation all around. It's the times we're living in now.

Most corporations perceive federal mandates to be important in the recruitment and hiring of women and minorities. However, these corporations vary in the significance they attach to EEO/AA. Corporations in this study admitted that EEO/AA legislation made a difference in implementing and managing diversity initiatives. In fact, in most cases, EEO/AA operates as an invisible hand; that is, EEO/AA are clearly felt even though their practices and behaviors are not identified under the banner of "diversity." Because of its compliance effect, EEO/AA continue to provide the foundation on which the recruitment and hiring of women and minorities is built. In fact, more so than ever, with tort law reform and other political efforts designed to protect the corporation's role and place in the economy, Affirmative Action programs can be viewed as the guardian of Equal Opportunities. Motivated by government policy or corporate interests, what is at stake is a greater representation of women and minorities in America's information technology industries.

It cannot be understated that legal sanctions and public scrutiny play an important role in the adoption of diversity strategies. Unlike Equal Employment Opportunity and Affirmative Action, diversity efforts are used as strategic defenses in order to reduce or minimize risk to allegations of discrimination resulting in possible lawsuits. Historically, legal sanctions and public scrutiny associated with employment discrimination claims have established precedents within corporations. In turn, corporations are encouraged strongly to implement strategies in response to vulnerability to legal action and negative public opinion.

On the other hand, government policy can result in unfavorable consequences for women and minority job candidates. By its very nature, the H-1B visa program, which is quite popular among information technology corporations, is a potential barrier to entry into the information technology labor force for U.S.-born individuals, especially women and minorities. In fact, it is a legalized means of denying women and minorities access to employment and career opportunities. In the final analysis, the representation of women and minorities in information technology corporations may hinge on political forces, particularly as it relates to foreign workers and the H-1B visa program.

Of great concern to me as a university professor is the possibility that college students, in response to corporations' preference for foreign workers in information technology industries, will opt themselves out of science and engineering fields and enter fields where career opportunities are brighter, such as law and business. Noticeably, over the past several years, major universities have reported that science and engineering majors enrollments have decreased, resulting in an overrepresentation of foreign-born students in these fields.

As for public policy, it is important to note that Affirmative Action's backlash is not only about its unpopularity as a political program, but also that many of its opponents seek to provide evidence of its ineffectiveness. Research findings are quite conclusive that the government's role is paramount in providing equal opportunities for women and minorities (Herring and Collins 1995; Heckman and Payner 1989). As for researchers who argue that government policies have played a trivial role in women's and minorities' advancement in the workplace, they fail to consider the effects of employment opportunities that sprang directly from federally funded welfare and community service organizations that coincided with civil rights protests in the 1960s. In fact, civil rights activities in the 1960s stimulated more heavily the federal governments' efforts to establish equal employment opportunity laws which were established as early as the 1940s (Collins 1997).

Despite President Bush's arguments in the State of the Union address in 2005, the absence of legal sanctions and negative public opinion regarding the hiring of women and minorities is troubling to me. Given that discrimination still exists and is accompanied by hate, prejudice, and perceived threat, it is virtually impossible for true equality to exist in the workplace. Legal sanctions and public scrutiny have contributed greatly to women's and minorities' entry and advancement in corporations. Government policy, especially Equal Employment Opportunity and Affirmative Action, is linked to modern-day diversity initiatives. This relationship demonstrates the dependency and fragility of women and minorities within federal policy and corporate strategies.

At the heart of this discussion throughout this chapter is a characterization of diversity as influenced by federal policy, legal decisions, and political activity. Taken together, legal pressures and political choices are important factors in explaining the complexity and challenges associated with the adoption of diversity strategies. An important piece of the puzzle, legal pressures and political choices, sheds light on the environmental forces that drive corporations to develop strategic initiatives focused on women and minorities.

Chapter Five

Social responsibility isn't a deep shift because it's a voluntary tactic. A tactic, a reaction to a certain market at this point. And as the corporation reads the market differently, it can go back. One day you see Bambi, next day you see Godzilla.

—Elaine Bernard, Executive Director of the Labor and Worklife Program at Harvard Law School and a prominent member of the Democratic Socialists of America

Chapter Five
HBCU: Help or Hindrance?

Having discussed my findings and analyses with my dearest friend Dawn, I was warned about readers' interpretations and conclusions. As a graduate of Spelman College, her concern about this chapter is that only one side is presented—that of the corporation. She is worried that my results may be misunderstood and misinterpreted. Because the historically black college and university (HBCU) experience is uniquely different from that experience in predominantly white colleges and universities, Dawn claims that this experience isn't easily understood without actually attending one of the nation's one hundred five HBCUs.

Dawn believes that those representing "white" corporations tend to measure their experiences with HBCUs against those of predominantly white colleges and universities. Inevitably, here lies a problem. Understanding Dawn's concerns and her unique perspective on my work, I do face a rather daunting challenge. For it is not my intention to show our nation's preeminent historically black colleges and universities in a negative light, but rather it is to provide insight on corporations' perceptions of their experiences with these institutions as a primary means for attracting and hiring women and minority talent. And so, I proceed here with caution.

As discussed earlier, the perceived influence of legal and political environments have become a characteristic feature of corporations that adopt diversity strategies; so too have interorganizational relationships.

Today, more so than ever, strategic alliances and partnerships with national organizations and colleges and universities provide the private sector with the human capital necessary for ensuring competitive advantage and productivity in the global economy. This chapter explores and characterizes recruitment strategies geared toward attracting women and minorities into the information technology corporation. Specifically, our discussions focus on the relationships among information technology corporations, HBCUs, and women and minority science and engineering associations. At the heart of my analyses is resource dependency—that is, interorganizational ties that are essential to the survival of the corporation. They simply cannot function alone or without cooperation from other organizations.

Resource Dependency

Faced with environmental conditions such as uncertainty and instability, the resource dependence model posits that an organization is not capable of generating all the various resources that it needs. Therefore, organizations are dependent on the environment for key resources such as raw material, finances, personnel, services, or production—simply put, significant resources that the organization does not perform or provide for itself (Hall 1999). What is important here are the *decisions* that the organization makes. Central to this premise is that *decisions* are made within the internal political context of the organization (Schreyogg 1980) and they deal with environmental conditions faced by the organization. An important aspect of the resource dependence model is that organizations attempt to deal actively with the environment. They manipulate the environment to their own advantage. Rather than operating as passive recipients of environmental forces, organizations will make strategic choices about adapting to the environment (Aldrich and Pfeffer 1976; Pfeffer and Salancik 1978). The role of management, of course, is vital to this process.

Because the sources of resources in the environment may be other organizations, resource dependence can be thought of as *interorganizational* resource dependence. In other words, this collaboration indicates that organizations rely on other organizations to provide vital resources to thrive and survive. It is necessary to note that a key dimension of resource dependence is *strategic choice* (Chandler 1962; Child 1972). This notion suggests that organizations make decisions from among a set of alternatives in regard to the strategy that the organization will use in its dealings with the environment. Moreover, the assumption is that the environment does not force the organization into a situation in which no choice is possible. Hence, the organization is faced with other possible alternatives in dealing with the environment. There is never only one choice. In this view, I assert that a characteristic of information technology corporations adopting diversity strategies is that they enter into interorganizational relationships. Specifically, that they work closely and develop partnerships with major suppliers of women and minority talent. Based on this assumption, I examine corporations' relationships with HBCUs and women and minority science and engineering associations.

The Historically Black College and University

Since the implementation of Affirmative Action programs in the late 1960s, HBCUs have emerged as fertile grounds for corporate recruiters. Over the past few decades, corporate America has sought talented individuals enrolled in HBCUs to fill challenging job positions. In fact, some studies suggest that students who attend HBCUs are typically more professionally oriented and mature than those drawn to majority institutions (Sturm and Moroh 1994). Such an orientation may certainly lead to a preference for majors in the scientific and engineering disciplines such as computer science and other technology related fields of study (National Science Foundation 1998). Today, HBCUs represent nearly 30 percent of all underrepresented groups entering the information technology labor force. The impact of the HBCU in this sector is quite significant.

Data collected by the National Science Foundation (2001) indicate that HBCUs have developed strategic approaches to motivate students to declare majors in IT related fields of study. Consequently, the proportion of these majors enrolled in HBCUs differs significantly from those at predominantly white colleges and universities. On average, between 1989 and 1996, HBCUs granted twice as many degrees in computer science than did majority institutions. Moreover, a relatively large number of students attending majority institutions that are attracted to and express an interest in information technology disciplines do not complete their degrees in such fields. As I discussed in Chapter 1, explanations for the difference in the number of science and engineering degrees granted to whites and African Americans in both types of institutions lie perhaps *not* in the profiles of their students, but rather in the ways in which the institutions attract and retain students in information technology disciplines.

Let's recap some important insights presented in Chapter 1 concerning the role of the "pipeline model" in HBCUs and predominantly white colleges and universities. To understand what HBCUs are doing differently to produce minority students in information technology majors, let's consider the role and impact of the pipeline model. The National Research Council claims that majority institutions implement the pipeline model by having students navigate certain barriers that are designed to filter out individuals who are incapable of attaining the higher levels of scientific knowledge. Students who remain in the pipeline are expected to enter into the scientific and technical professions and to do well.

On the contrary, the pipeline model is used quite differently in the HBCU. Instead of "filtering" students, the HBCU model stresses inclusion. This means that extensive outreach, mentoring, and support are key elements. Students are not left to fend for themselves; a supportive environment within the institution as well as among peers is fostered. When students experience academic difficulties, intellectual, emotional, and academic supports are made available. Studies indicate that the HBCU model, especially the mentoring component, is also effective in attracting and retaining women in science and engineering majors (Sturm and Moroh 1994; Walker and Rodger 1996).

Therefore, it is easy to assume that corporations attempting to increase their proportions of women and minorities would benefit from establishing partnerships with HBCUs in that they are a repository of specialized technical and scientific knowledge. However, as revealed in this study, the relationship between many corporations and HBCUs has *changed*. HBCUs are no longer perceived as a *preferred* source of women and minority talent. In fact, corporations are becoming less and less dependent on HBCUs to provide a diverse talent pool. They are seeking alternative choices in order to meet their critical needs for highly qualified and well-trained professionals.

Despite these popular and convincing reasons for recruiting at HBCUs, many corporations argue that organizational ties with them are *not* a very effective means of recruiting women and minority talent. In fact, corporations report common experiences with HBCUs. Furthermore, there are several factors contributing to corporations' resistance and reluctance to enter into and maintain interorganizational relationships with many of these colleges and universities.

Exorbitant Costs

A major concern of recruiting at HBCUs is the exorbitant *financial costs* associated with doing so. Corporations' growing disdain for recruiting at HBCUs is inextricably tied to their perceptions of their role as *financiers*. One senior HR executive characterizes the relationship between the corporation and HBCUs in the following way: "You know, it's like they hold corporate America hostage!" Faced with significant financial burdens, corporations realize that HBCUs are likely to charge as much as four times the amount required by majority institutions to participate in university recruiting activities such as job fairs. However, the high cost of participating in campus job fairs is only one aspect of corporations' frustrations with recruiting at many HBCUs.

There is widespread feeling among corporations that HBCU job fairs *vary* in terms of *quality*. Eighty-three percent of corporations in this study insist that some HBCU job fairs fail to meet industry standards. Inadequate space, poor planning, and low student participation are factors associated with negative views about HBCU job fairs. On the other hand, some HBCUs provide adequate resources and the necessary infrastructure to ensure the smooth operation of campus job fairs. Put simply, some HBCUs are better prepared than others to receive and host corporate sponsors. One interviewee, Sonya, a senior human resources manager, put it this way:

> The costs to participate in their recruitment activities are two, three, four times more expensive. And then you pay for

advertising on top of that [...] plus you pay to be a sponsor as well. Some of the schools do it very, very well and you get the bang for your buck. But there are other schools that do not. I have seen that impact of the financial barriers to companies getting in there [...] they will participate, though, maybe because diversity is important to them.

In corporations where recruiting budgets vary from year to year, meaning from higher to lower levels, frustrations center not only on the high costs attached to participating in campus job fairs, but also on the negative attitudes shown by HBCUs toward corporations that decline to participate in campus job fairs. Certain HBCUs tend to tarnish the corporation's established reputation of corporate giving and philanthropy though "word of mouth" bashing in higher education and corporate circles. As observed by Sonya:

> To participate in their recruitment fairs is tremendously expensive. The cost of entering is very expensive. And they're fickle. If you come one year and don't come the next, they kind of turn your picture to the wall. If you drop them one year because business has turned bad—and of course we all go through that—then all of a sudden you're in a *non gratis* position. They [HBCUs] won't hesitate to spread the word about your corporation and how it fails to "do the right thing."

There are additional factors that discourage relationships with HBCUs. Eighty-seven percent of corporations contend that the process of recruiting at HBCUs is labor intensive and requires a great deal of money, time, and commitment on the part of the corporation. When assessing the impact of corporate finances and time commitments required for recruiting at HBCUs, many corporations report that there is little to no return on their investments. Often, the corporations' recruitment efforts do not result in the identification or attraction of actual job candidates. Students do not express sincere interest in employment opportunities and rarely do they spend substantive time with recruiters. In addition, it is unlikely that interviews take place on campus, and the collection of resumes is usually a matter of protocol rather than actually reviewing each individually. Here is how one interviewee, Michael, a senior human resources manager describes his observation:

> The relationships are very expensive and the relationships take a tremendous amount of effort on the corporation's part. They don't always necessarily lead to the best recruiting. I have found—and this is my experience, so my personal opinion— that there's a huge expectation on the part of those historically black universities in particular that a corporation is going to just pour tons of money into that university, and there are really no guarantees that that is going to be a reciprocal relationship. That just is the cost of doing business, the cost of entry. And you've got to work that year in and year out.

Time

The notion and use of *time* by corporations differs considerably compared to its utility by HBCUs and higher education institutions in general. In fact, that old saying is appropriate here: *Time is money.* Many corporations perform services comparable to those offered by their majority competitors. That is, corporations compete for the best and the brightest and there are times when they do compete for the same individual. Efforts focused away from hiring highly qualified and well-trained individuals at a reasonable and competitive cost are viewed as a waste of time and an unnecessary burden on the corporation. On the contrary, colleges and universities ascribe to time primarily in terms of academic and teaching schedules that fall during certain seasons of the year—fall, winter, and spring. Time, then, has very little to do with the institution's bottom line. For higher education institutions, time pressures and restraints rarely impact their ability to compete among their peers, given that there is no profit-driven or bottom-line agenda. For example, it is not unusual for academic departments to consider and pursue their interests in creating new programs for several years. This would not be the case for corporations. Timothy, an interviewee in this study and a vice president for corporate diversity, offers these comments on the high costs and excessive time commitments associated with recruiting at HBCUs:

> We'll [corporations] try recruiting at these HBCUs and we see the cost associated with it [...] we won't initially get the return that we think we need. You can't go into these schools and pay double at a career fair and expect to hire ten people. It takes a very long time to establish the relationship with them. And, often, many recruiting departments don't have time to wait.

Recognizing that time is indeed a factor in recruiting at HBCUs, 79 percent of corporations claim that, on average, it takes a minimum of three to five years to experience a steady flow of students into the corporation. This is considered a relatively fair amount of time indicating a substantive investment on the part of the corporation as well as the college or university. However, the complaints about time in many corporations have much to do with their perceptions of how difficult it is to work with some HBCUs. Many of these colleges and universities are perceived as failing to demonstrate a capacity and commitment to work cooperatively with corporations.

Representation

Corporations report that certain HBCUs have staff members who do not represent the college or university's best interests. Personality types and attitudes are perceived as interfering with appropriate organization practices geared to engage and solicit corporate involvement. Several corporations are uncomfortable with existing structures purposed to respond to and interact with them. Offices and departments authorized by the college or university to work with corporations are considered to be inapt for developing and maintaining university–corporate relations. Frustrations of corporate managers with HBCUs have led them to characterize the HBCU–corporate relations experience in one way: HBCUs are *recipients* solely of corporate sponsorship and good will. And, they do not offer much in return. Michael sums it up this way:

[Referring to working with HBCUs] I don't think most corporations, except in some instances, always need to see immediate results, but it's got to be *easy* to work with, it's got to be easy to do business with, there has to be at least a give and take both ways. I think at some of the schools it simply hasn't been that way. It has been very difficult to work with them.

Competition

One of the most common beliefs among corporations is that HBCUs are no longer the exclusive and primary source of women and minority talent. Given many of their unfavorable experiences with them and the increased number of women and minorities majoring in information technology disciplines in majority colleges and universities, corporations are entering into more and more partnerships with predominantly white colleges and universities in hopes of hiring qualified and well-trained talent. Walter captures this sentiment:

You have really got to make a huge commitment to the HBCU and then you may not even get anything out of it. So what I think a lot of corporations have done is they've said look, there are a lot of great universities out there, and they have large minority populations. And again, we're all going after the same people and they are in limited supply, so you've got to branch out; there's no way you should put all of your eggs in one basket in this game. For instance, University of Michigan—fabulous engineering school, high minority population—is a great place to recruit. Chances of you picking up one or two there are almost better and less costly than having this huge relationship with Prairieview and Howard Universities.

Contrary to popular belief, many corporations have quietly shifted their focus and attention to recruiting women and minority students from non-HBCU institutions. In fact, recruitment decisions are not made lightly. Where corporations decide to recruit and their level of involvement requires formal decisions and approval from senior management.

The vast majority of corporations agree that it is *easier* to recruit at predominantly white colleges and universities despite the small numbers of women and minorities enrolled in science and engineering majors.

Corporations' lessened dependency on federal contracts and compliance with Affirmative Action has consequences for recruiting at HBCUs in particular. The emphasis and broadened desire to develop and maintain itself as a global organization permits the corporation to forego its longstanding history with many HBCUs. The political environment especially no longer requires or expects corporations to use HBCUs' unique status among American colleges and universities as primary suppliers of women and minorities. On the other hand, corporations' efforts to recruit at non-HBCUs provide opportunities to shape and influence the kinds of structures and practices associated with hiring recent and prospective graduates. Without the perceived limitations of federal policies and racialized programs, corporations have a greater chance of assimilating college and university structures to mirror those of their own, therefore increasing their chances to become key players in the life span of the institution.

Over 60 percent of corporations argue that recruitment at non-HBCUs leads to acquiring better qualified and well-trained employees. The suggestion that students who attend HBCUs and major in science and engineering are somewhat less prepared than those graduating from non-HBCUs is quite familiar. For years, many members of the higher education community have maintained that students educated at HBCUs lacked competitive skills and preparation for entry into corporate America. In her interview, Diane, a senior vice president, states:

> From a diversity and a female perspective, we have kind of mixed results in terms of do we go to HBCUs in the South to target the overall population, or do we go to a school like University of Michigan or Purdue or Carnegie-Mellon and target the diverse student populations at those schools. Although there is a smaller number of minorities, but maybe the overall credentials of those students that are there are going to be higher than the overall academic standards of an HBCU school? We're really trying to figure this out now. But so far,

we've had pretty good results recruiting diverse students from non-HBCUs.

Students who graduate from colleges and universities whose structures, behaviors, and cultures reflect those of the corporation are more likely to "fit" the corporate model of an ideal employee. The milieu of non-HBCUs is more likely to pave the way for students' adaptation to white-dominated work environments. Indeed, recruiting for diversity at non-HBCUs would be *easier* given minimal and insignificant differences in corporate–university practices, processes, and expectations. Simply put, corporations' pursuit of women and minorities at non-HBCUs eliminates many difficulties and frustrations resulting from different ways of managing and operating work organizations.

Concerns about HBCUs' motivation to establish relationships with corporations are reflected in companies' perceptions about a college or university's role in securing competitive jobs for its students. Eighty-six percent of corporations believe that most HBCUs demonstrate a stronger commitment to ensuring corporate giving than to nurturing corporate–university partnerships geared toward increasing the number of women and minorities in American corporations. Many corporations point out that an overemphasis on securing funds runs the risk of compromising the best career opportunities for students. This perception that HBCUs are limited in their use of corporate relationships is a serious one. It is a common thread that brings together corporations' explanations of HBCUs' behaviors. That is, the concern with financial sponsorship has overshadowed any and most prospects of long-term and substantive opportunities for influencing and shaping colleges and universities' structures and behaviors. One interviewee, Elizabeth, is a senior vice president for human resources and is very passionate about this perception:

> I don't know that they're really serving their student body as well as they could, because I don't think they're always keeping them in mind as their first customer, their client. I think they're a little bit more worried about their coffers than they are about whether or not their students are really getting access to the best opportunities out there. In some ways I think they exclude

corporations from wanting to participate, and therefore I think they close off some of those opportunities that might otherwise come to their campus for their students.

Yes, I think they're [HBCUs] more concerned about their coffers than their students and the opportunities that are presented to their students. I think that they kind of shoot themselves in their own foot…. They've [HBCUs] got something that the corporations want […] so, let's make them pay, and so that will make our university stronger and our coffers will be more.

Leadership

One issue that complicates further corporations' relationships with HBCUs is their perception of college leadership. Nearly 75 percent of corporations view many HBCU presidents as demonstrating poor leadership in this area. Specifically, they claim that senior-level administrators fail to understand corporate fundraising and strategic partnerships. HBCUs do not network well with corporations. They often are inclined to designate inappropriate departments, such as college career services and career planning counselors, to work with and nurture relationships with senior corporate managers.

Further, these departments are not concerned with developing long-term strategies with corporations but rather are purposed to solicit funds and sponsorships for the college or university. Frequently, corporations experience negative attitudes and resistance to corporate ideas, practices, and plans associated with their presence on campus. Hostility and volatile behaviors from college and university personnel create an environment in which anticipated alliances and partnerships cannot be t forged. These perceptions may result from individuals' issues associated with institutional power and turf. And, the fact that no sanctions exist to remedy corporations' negative views contributes to their anxiety and difficulty in working with certain HBCUs. Referring to his experiences over the past few years, Walter recalls in his interview:

Well, we need to be at Howard University, for example, because we want to be a good corporate citizen and they're an HBCU in our region. But trying to deal with them from a logistical and an easy-to-do-business-with standpoint is very, very difficult. I am referring to the *people* and the commitment of the people. Even at some of the traditional or predominantly white colleges, there are career centers, there are people in important positions that corporations deal with on an ongoing basis. There are a number of schools out there that have the wrong people in those positions, what I'll call the "old school" people. I think some HBCUs are very difficult to work with just from a people standpoint.

However, several corporations identify a couple of HBCUs—Morgan State and Florida A&M—that get the gold star for developing and nurturing relationships with corporate America. They credit university presidents. Many corporations claim that university presidents, not their designees or lower-level officers, are responsible for forging and maintaining positive relationships with them. One senior manager argues that Florida A&M is a model institution in this regard: "The president at the time, James Humphrey, really knew how to fundraise. He understood corporate culture. It's been my experience that very few HBCU presidents *really* understand corporate culture and fundraising."

Fundraising, as a skill, requires that university presidents invest time and energy in creating ways to invite corporations to explore opportunities to *invest* in their college or university. This ability to fundraise goes far beyond soliciting sponsorships and finances with no return on the investment. Corporations' influence on college and university campuses range from building large and important facilities, to establishing laboratories, to funding research, and to becoming instrumental in the development of the curriculum and instruction. This is especially true for areas such as science and engineering. The capacity to invest in human capital begins with the college and university president. It is at this level that the opportunities and relationships emerge. This is not always the case at many HBCUs. Many corporations believe that HBCUs are only interested in the corporate practice of signing over large checks with no strings attached.

The Economy

The impact of the economy on the corporation is yet another barrier to recruiting at HBCUs. During hard economic times, corporations are forced to minimize their financial support to external organizations. Hence, recruitment activities such as participation in job fairs are often suspended. Ninety-four percent of corporations maintain that, especially during economic downturns, HBCUs should keep in mind that the pursuit of job opportunities for their students—not financial sponsorships—is primary. Thus, in order to ensure the continued presence of corporations on their campuses, HBCUs should demonstrate greater flexibility and financial accommodations to corporations.

Many corporations perceive that HBCUs' focus on corporate sponsorship overshadows what is in the best interest of their students. Should corporations seek to be present on campus to implement activities such as career counseling, recruitment for summer jobs and internships, and future employment? If so, many HBCUs do not provide passage to corporations unless they pay dearly for it. In her interview, Elizabeth expresses her reservations about HBCUs' overall responsibility to students compared to their pursuit of corporate sponsorship:

> HBCUs must understand and have greater flexibility concerning corporations' [financial] good years and bad years; they should have a more welcoming environment for corporations [...] one that excuses the corporation from being a major sponsor but also allows the corporation to come and offer job opportunities to the students. The students are the ones that should be the winners in all of this. I'm not saying that there aren't other things to satisfy, such as fundraising goals, but at the end of the day I think placing the students from your university is really a big responsibility, and helping them. And I'm not sure that they're always helping them the best way that they could.

Nearly 80 percent of corporations that enter into periods of economic uncertainty find that the business area most heavily affected is human resources. Reducing labor costs for most corporations is a primary means of surviving economic hardship. As a strategic response to economic uncertainty, corporations tend to institute a freeze on hiring and terminate existing positions through layoffs and early retirements. Furthermore, recruitment efforts at American colleges and universities are usually interrupted or halted. Hence, HBCUs render themselves highly vulnerable to the suspension of corporate recruiting, given their preoccupation with securing corporate funding through job fairs and similar recruitment activities. One interviewee, Mark, a vice president of human resources, comments on how the economy affects not only the number of colleges and universities where recruiting occurs but also the estimated number of new college hires:

> Well, things have changed significantly for us because of the economy. Two years ago we were recruiting at close to one hundred colleges and universities and we had a formal university relations office. Right now we're recruiting overall at about 17 or 18 colleges. Two years ago, three years ago, our college numbers [new hires] were about 800. This year and last year our numbers were closer to 100. We've shifted from throwing out a wide net across the whole country to probably more regional in terms of a good number of schools in the Mid-Atlantic and Northeast, from Duke up through MIT and RPI.

Faculty

For those corporations that persist beyond the rudimentary career fair relationship, other recruiting efforts extend to establishing ties with HBCU faculty. Over half of corporations complain that faculty at HBCUs are absent from activities involving the potential placement of students in corporations. They argue that their lack of involvement in identifying and grooming students for competitive job opportunities is noticeable and unfortunate. Students who are interested in employment opportunities are perceived as having to fend for themselves. In general, corporations observe that students rarely receive help from professors with preparation for interviews, presentation of resumes, or references.

Furthermore, faculty's lack of participation in corporate-sponsored workshops, seminars, job fairs, and research activities is perceived as disregarding the opportunity to interact, network, and negotiate with representatives from the corporate sector. In fact, many corporations view their absence in most corporate activities as simply a demonstration of disinterest in what companies have to offer, not only to faculty but also to their students. For many companies, this is quite disturbing. Mark explains further in his interview:

> We invite faculty from a wide range of HBCUs to participate in industry workshops and seminars. We also offer, at little to no financial expense, training sessions for faculty introducing new and innovative technologies… you know, we view these as opportunities to build bridges and establish relationships with those individuals in the classroom. We also offer HBCU faculty internships and research opportunities with the corporation during the summer months. There has been little interest on the part of faculty to either learn more about what we can offer them or even their students. However, in the case of predominantly white colleges and universities, this is typically not the case.

The One-Shot Deal

In addition to qualms about the high costs and poor quality of career fairs, lengthy time commitments, negative attitudes, inflexibility, poor college leadership, and disengaged faculty members, many corporations frequently argue that recruiting for diversity at HBCUs is no longer a one-shot deal. In fact, recent corporate diversity strategies at HBCUs call for long-term and ongoing strategic approaches.

Although corporations' perceptions of recruiting experiences at HBCUs make it difficult to maintain substantive relationships, it is interesting to note that such experiences have led human resources professionals to reassess and revise their recruitment strategies. Because of negative experiences, corporations are choosing to slowly relinquish their traditional role as financiers and sponsor recruiting efforts focused on mentoring, internships, and corporate–university research partnerships. Hence, the process of recruiting HBCU students will occur over time rather than as a one-shot deal at local campus events. As corporations usher in new strategies for recruiting women and minority students, they report an interest in doing so at a smaller and select group of HBCUs. According to Sharon, a director of diversity in this study:

> It's not a one-time thing. It's a combination of ongoing relationships; there's no one-time activity. So obviously some of the best relationships, if you want to talk about strategies that work, are again a long-time commitment to a school and a willingness to make the commitment of three to five years in a place where you're going to have consistency in that relationship. Then, you'll start to see the fruits of your labor. So having a career fair at a school that doesn't even know very much about your company in one year definitely is not going to get you good job candidates.

Some corporations acknowledge constraints to consistency in recruiting competitive students from HBCUs. They argue that long-term and ongoing recruitment strategies would permit the time necessary to strengthen ties with HBCUs as well as generate a wealth of desirable, competent, and competitive job candidates. Future diversity efforts at HBCUs will become more flexible and extensive as well as include faculty and current employees of corporations. For example, existing employees who are alumni of HBCUs will serve as recruiting agents for the corporation. Sharon explains further:

> So, we must develop strategies that address what we are going to do to develop relationships with professors. What are we going to do to develop relationships with the students? To get our name out there, we're going to have to make some hires, and then after we've made those hires, we have to make sure

those employees are happy with our company so that when they go back as alumni to that school, and are recruiting members—because we want to make sure that the people that we've hired go back to their colleges and do more recruiting—then they can talk about the wonderful job that they have at the company along with the great experience that they're having, and then they can serve as mentors on how students can succeed and become essential employees for that company. These are ongoing efforts; it's not a matter of a one-shot thing.

Unlike twenty years ago, corporations are no longer limited to recruiting a diverse talent pool from American colleges and universities. In fact, more and more corporations are focusing their attention on the growing number of women and minority science and engineering associations. Although there are at least twenty-five IT related academic disciplines offered in American colleges and universities, many of these disciplines are represented by at least one professional association.

Women and Minority Science and Engineering Associations

The overarching goal of women and minority science and engineering associations is to attract and retain diverse populations in information technology. These professional groups, through education, training, mentoring, and financial sponsorships, are vehicles for professionalizing women and minorities entering or currently working in information technology professions. These organizations may, in fact, be ideal resources for any science and engineering industry that seeks to increase diversity in its talent pool.

As my survey data reveal, corporations with diversity strategies have increasingly formed organizational ties to several women and minority science and engineering groups. Table 5.1 reports loadings for three rotated principal components extracted from a covariance matrix of twenty-nine women and minority science and engineering associations. The table reports one factor analysis for all women and minority associations. My findings on factor (1) show that all types of women and minority science and engineering associations—women, black, and other minority

TABLE 5.1
Rotated Principal Components Analysis of Women/
Minority Science and Engineering Associations

Women/Minority Science and Engineering Professional Association	Factor		
	(1)	(2)	(3)
American Association of Women Entrepreneurs	.206	.189	.727
American Indian Science & Engineering Society	.306	.406	.633
Association for Puerto Ricans in Science & Engineering	.594	.239	.592
Association of Muslim Scientists & Engineers	.498	.158	.542
Association for Women in Science (AWIS)	.396	.687	.115
Black Data Processing Association (BDPA)	.264	.495	.479
Black Engineer.com	.383	.801	.200
Black Geeks Online	.724	.325	.375
Catalyst	.825	.269	.360
Chinese Software Professionals Association	.658	.142	.526
Institute for Women & Technology (IWT)	.685	.607	.548
Korean American Scientists & Engineers Association	.905	.163	.265
Minority Science & Engineering Program	.531	.512	.427
Native Americans in Science	.610	.327	.577
National Action Council on Minorities in Engineering	.420	.545	.518
National Association for Minority Engineering Admin.	.411	.255	.675
National Association of Mathematicians (NAM)	.721	.346	.414
National Council of Black Scientists & Engineers	.477	.691	.116
National Network of Minority Women in Science	.554	.226	.665
National Society of Black Engineers (NSBE)	.132	.856	.240
National Technical Association	.878	.191	.201
Society for Advancement of Chicanos & Native American Science	.801	.217	.323
Society for Hispanic Professional Engineers & Scientists	.520	.661	.238
Society of Mexican American Engineers & Scientists	.814	.328	.251
Society of Women Engineers (SWE)	.504	.792	.284
Southeastern Consortium for Minorities in Engineering	.819	.200	.358
Women in Engineering Programs & Advocates Network	.446	.375	.538
Women in Technology (WIT)	.299	.619	.559
Eigenvalue	19.0	2.49	1.43
Variance Explained	32.3	53.9	73.9
Number of Firms	83	83	83

associations—score positively on this dimension. Generally, this suggests that corporations demonstrate a pattern of affiliation with a wide range of women and minority science and engineering associations.

Although somewhat statistically weaker and more ambiguous, factor (2) clusters black science and engineering associations, and factor (3) slightly distinguishes women science and engineering groups. Taken together, my data reveal that corporations do not target certain science and engineering associations while ignoring others, but recognize that they are all important sources for recruiting women and minority talent.

Advertisements

Corporations affiliated with women and minority science and engineering associations are certain about the nature of that affiliation. Nearly 80 percent of corporations are linked primarily to these groups through the procurement of advertisements. In this case, there is no substantive relationship or full range of recruiting efforts with these organizations. These groups are simply avenues for publicizing employment opportunities and internships with the corporation. Surprisingly, some corporations are not interested in developing long-term and ongoing relationships with these groups. Since the 1990s, corporations have used these advertising opportunities to demonstrate a link to the association. This encourages the perception that the corporation is "diversity friendly" and a good corporate citizen. However, its involvement with many of the professional associations goes little beyond its printed image or logo in its advertisement. In his interview, Matthew provides a further explanation:

> More than likely, I'm going to buy advertising space on women and minority organizations' Websites versus trying to develop some sort of relationship because unfortunately my need is immediate, and I need to get candidates in here, and I need women and minority candidates. And I understand your vision statement, I understand what you want to do, but my need right now is to get someone on board *now*, and I don't have time to come to your meetings on a monthly basis, participate

and perhaps become a member of your board—I don't need all of that. I need to hire a qualified female or minority candidate.

Sponsorships

Similar to their experiences with HBCUs, over 75 percent of corporations express concerns about the high financial costs of doing business with women and minority science and engineering associations. However, despite such discontent, they recognize that there are benefits to sponsoring these organizations. Typically motivated by mandates and public approval, over half of corporations give annually to these professional associations. From a distance, demonstrated financial support shows that the corporation is in agreement with what the organization stands for, its mission, and purpose. However, financial backing can misrepresent behaviors and practices of the corporation. Sponsorship does not mean fair and equitable hiring decisions.

Because so many corporations choose to advertise in women and minority professional groups' printed materials and on their Websites, the corporation must gain an advantage by doing so. In fact, these advantages are multiple. In addition to perceptions of being a good corporate citizen, companies gain some political leverage as well. They associate sponsorship of women and minority professional groups with mandates such as Equal Employment and Affirmative Action practices. This calls into question their genuine and legitimate concern to wield their influence toward addressing the unique needs of women and minority professionals. Many human resources professionals comment on the sponsorship of women and minority science and engineering groups. For example, Stacy, a human resources senior specialist in this study, notes:

> I think that a lot of companies are willing to shell out, okay, $5,000 or $7,500 or $10,000 to say that, okay, we're partnering with the National Society of Black Engineers (NSBE); that comes out to be a check mark on the Affirmative Action program or the recruiting program, that we are a gold-level sponsor for the NSBE conference. But being able to truly see what your results are from that, I think, is a lot more long-term,

and I'm not sure why. But I want to stop far short of saying that I think the organizations are being opportunistic in trying to bring in funds, because I know in terms of running the events there's a lot of cost and a lot of time and a lot of money involved.

Other Recruitment Activities

Many corporations' recruitment strategies are not limited to organizational ties with HBCUs and women and minority science and engineering associations. Forty-two percent of companies participate in other distinguishing and common features of recruiting efforts focused on women and minorities. Although the processes and conditions under which recruiting efforts occur are important, a discussion of specific recruitment activities allows for a better understanding of what practices are associated with the adoption of diversity strategies. These activities provide a lens for examining what corporations actually do when "doing diversity."

Many corporations engage in a full spectrum of highly visible recruitment activities. As shown in Table 5.2, independent sample t-tests indicate that corporations with diversity strategies are hosting campus receptions and dinners, sponsoring campus workshops and seminars, and participating in campus job fairs. Corporations advertise in career magazines, on campus Websites, and in newspapers where they regularly offer internship and cooperative opportunities. In addition, they target women- and minority-serving colleges and universities and obtain personal referrals from faculty members, current employees, and key players in the industry and government sectors. These companies indicate that they serve on college governance boards and sponsor school-to-work transition programs. In essence, they do it all. The adoption of diversity strategies, then, implies that there are a host of activities associated with recruiting women and minorities. This, of course, does not mean that these activities will prove successful (as is the case with recruitment efforts at HBCUs). But they are visible and documentable and can be used to turn attention away from corporations' practices of inequality and discrimination.

TABLE 5.2
**Recruitment Activities for Women and Minority Job Candidates
on Adoption of Diversity Strategies (% Yes)**

Independent Variable	Firms with Diversity Strategies	Firms without Diversity Strategies	t
Host Dinners & Receptions for Professional Groups	40.0	25.0	1.584
Sponsor and Conduct Workshops at Professional Meetings	38.6	32.6	.602
Participate with Science & Engineering Societies	71.1	30.1	4.284***
Contribute Financially to Professional Societies	50.0	25.0	2.598***
Advertise in Magazines, Websites, Newspapers, etc.	64.4	46.1	1.817*
Personal Referrals from Key Players in Industry	81.8	75.0	.799
Personal Referrals from Current Employees	95.5	90.0	1.003
Participate with Local Community Groups	61.3	36.5	2.478**
Establish Training Programs with Other Organizations	41.8	17.3	2.647***
Work Collaboratively with the U.S. Military Branches	60.0	23.0	3.949***
Serve on Professional Associations Governance Boards	51.1	21.1	3.186***
		30.1	4.284***
Total Number of Firms			
Diversity Strategies	*45*		
No Diversity Strategies	*52*		

*Significant at the p < .10.
**Significant at the p < .05.
***Significant at the p < .01.

When I examined these practices under a more rigorous statistical method, several recruitment practices do not remain statistically significant. However, as shown in Table 5.3, there are some recruitment practices that show robust effects on the adoption of diversity strategies. Practices most indicative of diversity strategies are partnering with K–12 schools, obtaining referrals from current employees and key players in the industry and government sectors, serving on college governance boards, and sponsoring college-to-work transition programs.

However, Table 5.3 also shows that the effects of other recruitment practices, such as sponsoring activities on college and university campuses and targeting women- and minority-serving colleges and universities, are reduced in multivariate analysis. In particular, my survey findings bolster earlier explanations of corporations' experiences of recruiting at HBCUs. In contrast, they indicate that *networks* are the most significant interorganizational conduits of diversity strategies. Simply put, establishing partnerships that involve common interests, goals, and practices is key to "doing diversity." Employee referrals, especially, are becoming a preferred method of recruiting women and minority talent. Corporate recruiters do not have to leave the office. Referral bonuses encourage employees to identity qualified and well-trained candidates who are likely to be a good fit with the corporation. Mark expresses his preference for employee referral programs in his interview:

> I think the people who work for the organization probably know the needs and are probably in a better position than anyone else to identify people who are going to do well within the organization. So a lot of times they're picking someone who they feel can survive. And of course they're going to look like them. And if the bonus is big enough, you will be able to find them.

In sum, although corporations' concerns and criticisms of HBCUs are directly aimed at the conditions associated with their recruiting practices, corporations best capture the attitudes and behaviors of university administrators, staff, and faculty. Rarely do they mention concerns about the academic preparation and training of HBCU students. Corporations'

Table 5.3
Logistic Estimates for Recruitment Activities for Women/Minority Job Candidates on Diversity Strategies

Additional Variable	Firm Size B(SE)	Firm Age B(SE)	Firm Revenue B(SE)	Additional Variable B(SE)	Model X^2	Pseudo R^2	Sample Size
Hosting Dinners & Receptions for Professional Groups	.126(.375)	.308(.387)	.239(.203)	.335(.540)	7.300	.086	81
Sponsor & Conduct Workshops at Professional Meetings	.181(.375)	.276(.392)	.235(.204)	.026(.513)	6.174	.074	80
Participate with Science & Engineering Societies	.276(.433)	.639(.427)	.122(.224)	1.821(.587)	17.603	.195	81
Contribute Financially to Professional Societies	.163(.385)	.468(.418)	.140(.213)	1.057(.537)[B]	10.179[B]	.119	80
Advertise in Magazines, Websites, Newspapers, etc.	.117(.379)	.435(.401)	.203(.208)	.558(.494)	8.200	.096	81
Referrals from Key Players in Industry	.200(.377)	.279(.392)	.237(.203)	.344(.562)	6.549	.079	80
Referrals from Current Employees	.191(.378)	.353(.393)	.268(.205)	.200(1.104)	7.991[A]	.095	80
Participate with Local Community Groups & Associations	.202(.386)	.379(.408)	.161(.211)	1.055(.491)[B]	10.922[B]	.128	80
Establish Training Programs with Other Organizations	.186(.391)	.433(.426)	.115(.216)	1.497(.616)	11.869[B]	.139	79
Work Collaboratively with the U. S. Military Branches	.025(.403)	.366(.426)	.183(.215)	1.653(.553)[C]	17.315[C]	.192	81
Serve on Professional Associations Governance Boards	.050(.389)	.247(.404)	.238(.209)	1.156(.552)[B]	11.176[B]	.132	79

[A]Significant at the p<.10   [B]Significnat at the p<.05.   [C]Significant at the p<.01.

frustrations with HBCUs are in direct response to administrative practices and political workings of the institution.

Several corporations admit candidly that many HBCUs employ the wrong people to interact with and engage them. From the college president to the career counselor, those with institutional responsibility for corporate relations are perceived to be the wrong people. As a consequence, corporations believe that they forfeit their position to ensure the best employment opportunities for their students. The inflexibility of HBCUs to cooperate with corporations suggests intentional practices and behaviors. Institutional and even cultural resistance to "white" dominated corporations and their preferred structures and behaviors are likely to frustrate and challenge companies to eventually seek other alternatives for predicting a consistent flow of information technology talent from other organizations.

Whether motivated by their own self-interest or driven by the moral imperative to do the right thing, many corporations are *changing* their strategic approach to recruiting at HBCUs, justifying such change in terms of efficiency, noting extraordinary savings in time and money. Toward this end, corporations are also turning inward and relying on employee networks to attract women and minority new hires. The political, legal, and even economic times allow corporations to enter and engage new and alternative ways of recruiting and hiring women and minorities. Diversity strategies, influenced by Equal Employment Opportunity and Affirmative Action practices, provide the impetus for strategically seeking out diversity. Therefore, when one strategy does not work, the corporation chooses to seek out another in order to meet its critical needs.

One does not have to draw intellectual conclusions about resource dependency to understand that the environment, be it social, political, or economic, is a significant force shaping the strategic choices of corporations. To put it plainly, the role of HBCUs as suppliers of a diverse talent pool is changing and the dependence is shifting to other sources—at least in part, majority institutions and current employees of the corporation.

The nature of the relationship between women and minority science and engineering associations and corporations is essentially financial. Characterized by corporate sponsorship of national conferences and the procurement of advertising space on Websites and in widely circulated publications, corporations' ties to women and minority professional groups has become an important source of good publicity rather than a valuable mechanism for attracting a diverse candidate pool. Frankly, many women and minority organizations are faced with the daunting task of raising funds to have professional meetings and conferences. Corporations, then, serve a vital role. On the other hand, corporations do benefit from favorable publicity associated with women and minority groups. Is this ultimately about a moral imperative to do the right thing—to be a good corporate citizen? Perhaps this *quid pro quo* behavior works for everyone. However, the misconception that there exists a real working relationship between these groups and the corporation tends to misinform individuals' perceptions of the work environment and policies that directly impact career opportunities of women and minorities. The old phrase "You can't judge a book by its cover!" is applicable here.

Finally, the very nature of corporations' relationships with women and minority organizations in general tends to reflect the value and significance of these organizations. Surprisingly, corporations fail to recall the relevance of HBCUs, at least historically, as a vital means of producing well-educated and well-trained women and minorities. What has happened now compared to the heyday of corporate recruitment at HBCUs in the '60s, '70s, and '80s? Have alleviated political pressures on corporations provided an escape route for them to alter their relationships with HBCUs? Nonetheless, the consequences of relinquishing organizational ties and instituting fundamental changes in recruitment strategies will be felt most severely by the next generation of young women and minorities pursuing careers in information technology.

Chapter Six

Some of the best creative minds are employed to assure our faith in the corporate world view. They seduce us with beguiling illusions. Designed to divert our minds and manufacture our consent.

—Anonymous

Chapter Six
The Many Faces of Diversity

O ver the past years, most corporations agree that diversity behaviors benefit the organization. In some way, they contribute to the overall desired outcomes of the organization. To understand better how diversity efforts benefit most corporations, it is important to recognize that there are underlying reasons or justifications that drive corporations to implement them. Rarely are corporate decisions to attract and retain women and minorities made in a vacuum. There is some motivation to do so. This discussion requires that I "bring the firm in" and explore those organizational perspectives, practices, and behaviors associated with adopting diversity strategies. To accomplish this, I provide a discussion of how corporations' perception of diversity is shaped by business, moral, and plural arguments.

The Business Face of Diversity

The most frequently cited justification for implementing diversity strategies is the business objective. Eighty-five percent of corporations argue that diversity is a good business strategy. In other words, corporations need diversity strategies to survive and thrive. Corporations situate their diversity strategies in their overall business objectives. In fact, to solidify formal diversity structures and behaviors, the vast majority of corporations have adopted distinctive, clear, and well-articulated written policies on diversity.

Corporations view the ability to communicate their commitment to diversity through their mission and vision statements as a serious and legitimate way of laying the foundation for the implementation of diversity practices. Some corporations argue that diversity statements are crucial because they reflect the importance of diversity not only outside the organization but also internally. Kerry, a senior human resources manager, explains in his interview:

> I think there needs to be a statement of commitment that is obviously verbalized for all in the corporation to see that we take this issue seriously, that we apply ourselves to the pursuit of whatever the vision of the mission may be. And I think without it it's kind of like a boat without an oar, or a boat without a rudder, because it just doesn't steer you any way unless you have it.

Many corporations claim that diversity statements are an effective tool for communicating the corporation's position on diversity. Interestingly, some corporations claim that these statements are vehicles for moving corporate leaders to clearly and consistently communicate the corporation's diversity goals. In her interview, Kimberly, a vice president for human resources, puts it this way:

> It's absolutely critical that there be a well-formulated strategy statement for a couple of reasons. One is so that leaders can have a common and consistent communication about diversity strategy, and the second is so that it can be clear to people what's important in terms of diversity.

The majority of corporations believe that leaders are crucial to adopting and implementing diversity initiatives. They, too, must embark upon their own personal journey in order to recognize and understand that the corporation's diversity practices are key to the organization's success. The corporation requires more than a nod toward diversity from its CEO.

The leader's ability to communicate well the corporation's vision of diversity is only the beginning. Beyond its articulation, CEOs must look for ways to mentor for diversity, challenge their peers to do diversity, and, more importantly, take risks necessary to move implementation forward. Otherwise, their smooth language and articulation of the corporation's diversity propositions may prove to be empty rhetoric for public consumption.

While some corporations view diversity statements as an important tool inside the corporation, others claim that they are equally important externally. Considered central to marketing strategies, diversity statements attract people—both employees and customers—who value and appreciate organization efforts geared toward inclusion. One interviewee, Martha, a senior vice president for diversity, stated:

> Many of our customers and prospective hires are concerned about our diversity plans. Our customers are now asking us what we are doing in terms of diversity. We are now including information specifically on our diversity programs. Yes, the interest in our diversity pursuits is growing and growing among our key constituents.

Because formal, written statements are viewed as solidifying the corporation's commitment to diversity, such perceptions can form the basis of recruitment and hiring decisions. However, diversity statements, just as mission and vision statements, are espoused values of the corporation. They are stated strategies, goals, and beliefs about what seems to work best for the company, as shown by the following examples:

> "In respecting and valuing the diversity among our employees and all those with whom we do business, managers are expected to ensure that there is a work environment free of all forms of discrimination and harassment."

> "We believe that diversity enriches our performance and products."

Or, "As a global company touching diverse customers and markets wherever we do business, we value individual perspectives. We recognize that it is just and right to treat every human being and their culture with decency and respect."

Like these statements, mission and vision statements are useful in assessing the corporation's position on a particular issue. They provide insight into what corporate leaders and managers might say in many situations. However, they are not very useful in predicting what the corporation might *do*. That is, the espoused values of the corporation are idealized and not necessarily based in corporate practices and behaviors. Hence, diversity statements, although most often linked to the mission and vision of the corporation, may serve as window dressings that adorn the corporate suite.

Indeed, the business case for diversity extends well beyond affirmative statements and written declarations about inclusion in the workplace. The famous *Workforce 2000: Work and Workers for the Twenty-first Century* identified the changing gender and racial/ethnic composition of the workforce as a major trend in the economy. This report almost single-handedly is responsible for the nation's fascination with and urgency to implement formal and official diversity structures in corporate America. The report's conclusion indicates that by the year 2000, only 15 percent of individuals entering the workplace would be American-born white males compared to 47 percent in 1987. Certainly, these projections captured the attention of American businesses and consequently made managing diversity a bottom-line issue. It is at this juncture that diversity strategies became linked to diverse customers and markets, which in turn were believed to contribute to corporate profitability and productivity.

An overwhelming 95 percent of corporations recognize the importance of understanding cultural nuances of diverse populations in that it allows them to tap into new and increasing markets. Demographic changes in the United States—that is, minorities' emergence as the majority population—are critical to increasing or even maintaining market share and attracting new employees. The growing awareness of the spending power of women and minorities has caused information technology corporations to recognize that the marketing, services, and sales of information technology products reflect the preferences of individuals' needs, wants, and styles. During the interview, one human resources manager explains:

> Diversity must be a priority if we want to continue to be a worldwide pillar of technology; if we want to remain number one, then we have to understand who our customers are. Therefore, to understand who are our customers, we have to have an employment base that can relate to various groups and to help us produce products that are going to be of interest to various groups. So it's full circle. We have to realize why diversity is an important part of our strategic goals, and even our products, why it's important to our employees and why is it important for us to be successful.

More recent population demographic data indicate that minorities are expected to compose 52.3 percent of the nation's population by 2043. This projection suggests a significant shift in the country's cultural, racial, and ethnic composition. Some U.S. states, for example, Texas, have already reached a "minority majority" status, where the number of single-race, non-Latino whites is lower than the population of other races and ethnic groups combined. California, the District of Columbia, Hawaii, and New Mexico are experiencing significant growth in minority groups (U.S. Census Bureau 2008). The same is true for women. More so than ever, it is anticipated that women will assume greater roles in corporations. Overall, these numbers are vital for corporations to, first of all, be aware of and, secondly, understand in terms of their business strategies. These demographic shifts are likely to impact corporations' marketing plans, retention of market shares, and efforts to employ the best well-trained, qualified individuals.

Sociologically speaking, significant demographic shifts will have an impact on the nation's social makeup. Until these shifts are realized, one can only anticipate cultural, social, and political change. And, the institution most likely to be greatly impacted is the American business. Corporations employing a significant base of diverse populations will be prepared to understand, socially and culturally, the nuances of various population sectors, enabling them to recognize and respond to new opportunities in the marketplace. To gain a unique understanding of the consistent growth influencing women and minorities, it is necessary to take a look at what is actually driving it.

It is projected that between 1990 and 2012 blacks will double their spending power. This assumption is not only based on projected population growth, but also the rate at which many blacks are advancing in their careers and creating their own businesses. Compared to whites, a larger proportion of blacks are entering the workforce for the first time and climbing the corporate ladder, further increasing their household incomes (Selig Center for Economic Growth Report 2007). While an average of 14 million black households in the United States spent an overwhelming 70 percent of the overall average household expenditure in the United States, there were a number of key areas in which blacks spent more, including telephone services, utilities, property rentals, clothing for young children, and footwear (Selig Center for Economic Growth Report 2007). These data are fundamental to corporations. By focusing on blacks' buying power in certain regions and category of expenditure, companies are able to identify opportunities to provide services to meet the unique preferences and needs of these markets.

Focusing on Latinos as a viable market, data indicate that they are the largest-growing segment among all minorities and the fastest-growing segment among all U.S. populations. Latinos are anticipated to more than triple their discretionary income between 1990 and 2012. Hence, the news is good for corporations. Together, blacks and Latinos represent a superb and consistent source of buying power.

Latinos have grown in population to 41.5 million, accounting for half the nation's population growth over the span of one year—between the period of July 2003 and July 2006 (U.S. Census Bureau 2007). This explosive growth in population is caused by higher birth rates and strong immigration numbers, with the highest proportion of immigrants coming from Mexico, Cuba, and El Salvador (U.S. Census Bureau 2000). A relatively large number of Latinos are benefiting from better job opportunities. Younger Latinos are entering the labor market at increasingly higher percentages and are earning increases in job responsibility and pay, which bolsters their buying power (Selig Center for Economic Growth Report 2007).

Culturally, corporations have gained significant knowledge in understanding the Latino market. For example, there are differences between acculturated, bicultural, and unacculturated Latinos. These categories also apply to many other immigrant groups. Acculturated Latinos consist mainly of those who are second generation or greater. They are comfortable speaking English at work or in social settings. Their values and perceptions are similar to the general U.S. population (Meadows 2004). Within this group, there is a trend toward retro-acculturation—the rediscovery of one's heritage—which has embraced cultural influences in food, music, and other elements of their Latino heritage. Bicultural Latinos have fully adapted to U.S. culture; however, many of them remain connected to their Latino heritage. They are comfortable speaking both English and Spanish and are exposed to both cultures. Most bicultural Latinos arrived in the United States at an early age and they continue to identify themselves with their parents' nationality (Meadows 2004). On the other hand, unacculturated Latinos consist of foreign-born Latinos who have recently arrived in the United States, usually as adults. Their primary language is Spanish and their affinity for products and services remains deeply rooted in their experiences in their Latin American homeland.

Of primary concern to corporations when dealing with immigrant groups is communication. It is important to understand that a group's cultural references and experiences affect their perception of products and in general, their buying decisions. Messages that will appeal to an acculturated individual may not be likely to do so to an unacculturated audience. Understanding and embracing culture, especially for large and complex groups of immigrants with buying power, is important to corporations. Such markets cannot be avoided due to ill-prepared structures that fail to communicate and respond to customer's preferences and needs.

Let's turn our focus to another minority group—Asian Americans. There are nearly 14 million people of Asian heritage living in the United States. Asian Americans represent East Asian nations such as Japan, China, and Korea and South Asian countries such as India, Pakistan, and Nepal. Southeast Asian countries include Thailand, Vietnam, and Malaysia (Meadows 2005). The Census Bureau estimates that 13.5 U.S.

residents are Asian American or Asian in combination with one or more other races, composing 5 percent of the total population. However, Asian groups represent a 5 percent surge in the population between 2000 and 2004 (U.S. Census Bureau 2005). California has both the largest population of Asians (4.6 million) and the largest numerical increase (367,100) since April 2000; in Hawaii Asians make up the highest proportion of the total population (58 percent) (U.S. Census Bureau 2005).

Asians are anticipated to double in population and spending power between 1990 and 2012. Like many other groups, they will benefit from the nation's economy. However, Asians in particular will benefit from greater education, which leads to employment or higher-level positions (Selig Center for Economic Growth Report 2005). Fifty percent of Asians age twenty-five and older have a bachelor's degree or higher level of education, compared to 27 percent of the total U.S. population. They are a higher proportion of college graduates compared to any race or ethnic group in the country. Eighty-eight percent of Asians age twenty-five and older are high school graduates versus 85 percent of the general population in this age group, and 19 percent possess an advanced degree such as a master's, M.D., or Ph.D. The corresponding rate for all adults in this age group is 9 percent (U.S. Census Bureau 2003). Continued strength in immigration among Asians and various subgroups is also positively impacting their buying power.

Data show that Asian spending power is geographically focused when compared to the overall customer market. In 2004, the ten states with the largest Asian consumer markets made up 63 percent of the national 77 percent of Asian buying power (U.S. Census Bureau 2004). Once again, it is imperative for corporations to identify areas where regional growth is occurring in order to pursue market opportunities.

Another minority group of the U.S. population that will increase in spending power is the Native American market. It is projected to grow by an astounding 54 percent in the period between 1990 and 2012—more than four times that of the general population (Selig Center for Economic Growth 2007). However, despite this fast-paced growth, the Native American population will increase only from 0.8 percent of the total population in 1990 to 1 percent in 2010 (U.S. Census Bureau

2005). This is the only ethnic market whose growth is not propelled by immigration but solely by birth rate.

Native Americans also benefit from more jobs and increased levels of entrepreneurship (Selig Center for Economic Growth Report 2007). Between 1997 and 2004, businesses owned by Native American women and Asian Americans each grew 69 percent. Still, Native Americans are expected to make up only 0.6 percent of U.S. buying power in 2012. This is up slightly from their share of 0.5 percent in 1990.

While women are not an "emerging" market, they are indeed an important sector. They are responsible for a striking 83 percent of all consumer purchases. Women generate about 55 million dollars annually in spending—about half the nation's gross domestic product (Barletta 2002). Minority women are a buying powerhouse. According to a 2004 report by the market research firm Packaged Facts, the combined group of blacks, Asians, and Latinas have grown nearly 40 percent between 1995 and 2003 versus the population of white women, which grew a mere 7 percent (U.S. Census Bureau 2003). These 32 million women hold approximately $725 billion in purchasing power and the report estimates that the total will exceed $1 trillion by 2011.

The Partridge Report (2009) estimates that the buying power of multi-cultural women is approximately $1.1 trillion. In fact, multicultural women represent 26 percent of the buying power of all U.S women. The buying power of multicultural women will increase at a faster rate than that of U.S. consumers as a whole because of the disproportionately rapid growth in the multicultural women's population. In 2014, multicultural women will control 28 percent of the buying power of American women, compared to 26 percent in 2009. Between 2000 and 2008, the population of multicultural women increased by around 7 million, while the number of non-Hispanic white women grew by only 3 million. Multicultural women accounted for 70 percent of the growth in the population of women in the United States during this period.

The impact of demographic population change has been heightened by the ability of corporations to recognize and respond to women's and minorities' buying power. Corporations' diversity strategies, then, are inextricably linked to new markets and their significant growth over short periods of time. In fact, many corporations are faced with the awesome challenge of securing these markets by competing for them. Many corporations find themselves improving productivity and quality by capitalizing on the talents and skills of employees that provide connections to new markets and customers—women and minorities.

More and more corporations recognize that the cost of a homogeneous workplace is great. Many corporations adopt diversity strategies, understanding that they are an essential investment. However, some corporations act as if it is financially prudent to cut or reduce costs associated with developing a diverse workforce—but it is also necessary to examine closely the costs associated with doing so. The fact that women and minorities represent an astonishing level of buying power in the marketplace requires corporations to implement strategies to build relationships and alliances with them. To fail to do so could result in a loss of competitive advantage.

A brief word about buying power. The nation's buying power—the total after-tax income available for spending on goods and services—is anticipated to increase by 159 percent by 2012. Despite its uneven growth in recent years and moderate recessions over the past decade, the gross domestic product—output of goods and services produced by labor and property located in the United States—is expected to increase moderately through 2012. Despite economic hardships such as home foreclosures and stifling gasoline and food prices, recent data show that the gross domestic product has increased at an annual rate of 1.9 percent (Bureau of Economic Analysis 2008).

In order to capitalize on emerging and untapped markets, corporations need employees who understand them. Cultural, racial, ethnic, and gender stereotypes, myths, biases, prejudices, and misconceptions are costly and lead to missed opportunities to acquire new markets and customers and, worse, may also lead to the high probability of offending existing customers. PepsiCo has found that fostering a greater understanding of customers adds generously to the company's bottom line. Studying ethnic markets leads to new products such as guacamole-flavored Doritos chips and Gatorade Xtremo, targeted toward Latinos, and Mountain Dew Code Red, which appeals to blacks. These additions to Pepsi's offerings added an estimated one percentage point of the corporation's 2003 revenue growth of 7.4 percent, about $250 million

(*Wall Street Journal* 2005). In addition to focusing on external markets, corporations' diversity strategies are linked to companies' employee-retention behaviors. With the amount of time and money involved in recruiting women and minorities, the failure to retain them results in a waste of resources. Therefore, the retention of these human assets is a corporate priority.

The business justification of diversity also involves the corporation's vulnerability to negative publicity. Publicity surrounding accusations of racism, sexism, or any form of discrimination against any group in the population can easily lead to customer alienation or even protests and boycotts. Criticisms of excessively high profits of a company can even cause share prices to decrease or destroy relationships with valued customers or employees who may feel betrayed by unfavorable policies and behaviors, comments, or any communication in opposition to an organization's culture that does not value or demonstrate diversity. Hence, the power of public opinion toward diversity and diversity issues can affect the company's bottom line.

As discussed in Chapter 4, several corporate leaders agree that their diversity initiatives are in place to assist in protecting the company from litigation. Those companies that fail to adopt strategies to diversify their workplace are placing themselves at risk for hefty attorney fees and fines. In 2004, the EEOC received slightly fewer complaints than they did a few years prior. However, forty lawsuits filed with the EEOC in 2004 cost corporate America nearly $75 million. Accompanied by negative publicity and even a wave of additional complaints, possible lawsuits are never good for the company's bottom line.

Strategies focused on diversity are also linked to the corporation's business objectives through the pursuit of human capital. Because corporations value diversity, they must cultivate a diverse employee pool. Here lie strategies to not only attract and hire women and minorities, but also to retain them. Although many corporations do agree that their most important asset is their people, they must do what is required to actually tap the human capital available to them. In fact, certain industries are quite reliant on innovation; this is the case for corporations who produce software products and services. Creativity, innovation, productivity, and efficiency come from capitalizing on, and even exploiting, human capital. Human capital, then, usually translates into success for most corporations. As Bill Gates stated, "Microsoft's only factory asset is the human imagination" (Peters 1992, 4). As a primary business objective, a diverse labor pool hinges on acquiring and developing human capital.

Being able to capitalize on untapped human resources leads to a corporation's capacity to gain and maintain competitive advantage. In other words, competitive advantage in the information technology world means that companies must acquire the ability and capacity to create and apply new technologies more rapidly and effectively than their competitors. This ability and capacity is greatly dependent on the skills of their workforce. Innovation is critical here, especially for corporations that are involved in creating, developing and applying new technologies. As noted by Elizabeth in her interview:

> Diversity means that the corporation can respond to the need for new and changing products to meet newly identified market segments. The more diversity we have, the more capable we are of maintaining our competitive advantage. We need employees that can flourish in diverse environments; we need their talents, genius and abilities to keep up with this new global economy.

At the heart of the business rationale for diversity is peak performance. As argued in resource dependence theory, an organization's ability to generate profits depends on their acquisition of specialized knowledge. In a profession-driven business like information technology, diversity strategies hinge on the acquisition of human capital—attracting, developing, and retaining it. Therefore, capitalizing on women and minority talent bolsters corporations' success in profits, productivity, competitive advantage, and innovation. Put another way, diversity, that is, women and minorities, is good for business.

During the 1970s and 1980s, public opinion about gender, racial, and ethnic discrimination shifted toward organizational efforts to create policies to ensure equal opportunities for women and minorities. However, in the 1990s the political winds of change were filled with complaints about hiring targets, quotas, and reverse discrimination. In a slew of Supreme Court cases, the political and social backlash against Affirmative Action programs was launched. Nonetheless, despite negative sentiments and attitudes toward certain legislation, mandates have profoundly shaped corporate views on diversity. These mandates have led to the transformation of American corporations from rationalizing the targeting of women and minorities through the rhetoric of Affirmative Action to justifying their pursuit through moral arguments.

The Moral Face of Diversity

Sitting at the Business-Higher Education Forum's roundtable on diversity was perhaps the most thrilling experience of my life as a graduate student. Composed of the nations' top CEOs and college and university chancellors and presidents, the Forum gathered one rainy afternoon in Seattle to talk about diversity. The focus was on the recruitment of U.S.-born women and minorities from America's colleges and universities into the nations' top corporations. Leaders from both the private and education sector debated the reasons for "embracing" behaviors to diversify their institutions. It was 2002, not 1960; who would imagine that such influential individuals would gather to discuss the reasons corporations and colleges and universities should care about diversity?

Most CEOs agreed that, indeed, the presence of women and minorities was especially important to their work environment. Recognizing their influence and power, rarely did chancellors and college presidents disagree with any position taken by members of the corporate elite. In this spirit, many college presidents claimed that there was much work to be done in their local communities and throughout their regions to produce better-educated minorities. Together, both groups emphasized the need for increased partnerships with K–12 schools and community colleges to attract and graduate women and minorities in important areas such as science and technology. However, using the argument of globalization, while many CEOs were deliberate about their commitment to capitalizing on the talents of women and minorities, they were also vehement that these groups must be well-educated, trained, and qualified for entry into the corporation.

As each individual around the table gave his or her own understanding of diversity and its relevance to their corporation, many CEOs offered a number of reasons for doing diversity. Interestingly, younger CEOs heading younger companies leaned toward the business case for diversity. However, in every instance, older CEOs responsible for guiding older corporations—especially those known as the diversity pioneers—offered a simple rationale: "It's just the right thing to do." Amidst arguments of globalization, competitive advantage, and human capital, moral arguments centering on the reparation of past injustices seemed to be the main focus. As such, the moral face of diversity was powerful. The moral face of diversity ended the discussion on a high note while silently setting a tone of equality and justice, both of which should resound in American schools and the workplace.

The case of implementing diversity strategies requires some convincing and persuasion. In response, moral arguments are heavily used to engender support of organization strategies that target women and minorities. In many American corporations, diversity is situated in ethical terms as *the right thing to do*. Influenced by the ideal of providing equal opportunities for historically oppressed groups, corporations now verbally acknowledge past injustices and inequalities and seek to correct them.

Shaped by a moral conviction or ethic to "do the right thing," corporations implement diversity strategies, in part, because they want to be perceived as *good corporate citizens*. That is, they seek to demonstrate social responsibility by helping solve social problems that adversely affect individuals, groups, and communities in society. Being a good corporate citizen usually entails advancing the social and economic well-being of others so as to ensure the development of their full potential and participation in societies.

Among corporations who advocate the moral relevance of diversity, establishing partnerships and alliances with women and minority organizations is a routine activity. Corporations justify such relationships by arguing that it is the right thing to do. Robert, a director of corporate diversity, comments, "We work with women and minority groups because we want to be good citizens; we desire to build strong relationships with the community. Why? It's just the right thing to do."

Compared to the majority of corporations, a small proportion, only 18 percent, use moral arguments to support their diversity strategies. It is important to mention that corporations who use moral arguments are *unlikely* to link diversity to their business objectives. Typically, corporations attach mandates, such as Equal Employment Opportunity and Affirmative Action, to their decision to do the right thing. In fact, some corporations associate compliance with being a good corporate citizen. During his interview Walter explains:

> Our relationships with women and minority organizations exist because we strive to be good corporate citizens and, you know, there is a compliance effect to doing so. The company tries to display the right attitude about women and minorities and be responsible to these groups. The law says we have to and we really want to ... so, we partner with minority-serving colleges and universities and other groups around the country.

Unlike the business rationale, the moral face of diversity relies on attitudes and beliefs rather than performance. Drawing their strength from broad societal principles of equality, fairness, and respect, moral arguments concerning diversity rest on the corporation's ability to demonstrate moral action. Hence, many corporations attach themselves to women and minority groups and institutions who, in turn, help promote their company as an ethically conscious institution.

Although moral arguments support the corporation's decision to implement diversity structures and behaviors, they do not address the trends of today's modern corporation of achieving competitive advantage by tapping into diverse groups. For those corporate executives that assert moral reasons for doing diversity, I am convinced that their diversity policies and practices are at greater risk for elimination because they are not linked to business objectives when times are hard or they are considered ancillary when times are good. Hence, the moral arguments of diversity are "nice" but not very sufficient for the long haul if a diverse workforce is to be realized. In fact, I am certain these arguments alone are not good enough to ensure that complicated issues related to the discrimination of women and minorities be resolved as painlessly as possible. However, I believe that perhaps moral arguments are best suited for home, church, communities, schools, and even private settings where their philosophical and ethical principles are not swayed by the varying attitudes and behaviors of employees and shareholders. Of each dimension of diversity, I contend that moral arguments are the most fragile and volatile.

The Plural Face of Diversity

What happens when the corporation reaches one of its very important strategic goals—to become a diverse workplace? There are some corporations that have achieved success in doing diversity. They continue to be successful at recruiting, hiring, and retaining an adequate number of women and minorities. All is good. Well ... not quite. Some corporations claim that seeking diversity is not the be-all end-all of an inclusive workplace. Once the work environment comprises diverse populations, there is great potential for problems. There is no guarantee that these groups, consisting of many individuals, will understand and respect each other but, more importantly, work cooperatively to achieve the organization's goals. For instance, in her interview, Susan, a senior vice president for human resources, recalls how her corporation experienced difficulties after achieving the company's diversity goals:

> Once we met our diversity goals, people began to have problems with each other based on individual differences. There was a great deal of competition and lack of unity among a large number of our employees. We had many disputes and complaints. We tried just about everything. Teams did not work. Senior management was ill-equipped to deal with all this. For a while, it was a fairly hostile environment where no one seemed to work well with their colleagues.

In essence, diversity, by its very nature, recognizes and values individual group differences. However, its challenge is to maintain a work environment that recognizes and values differences among individuals. As this study suggests, a corporation hires an African American female network engineer who has more in common with her white male senior manager (e.g., education, lifestyle, and professional interests) than she does with her African American female secretary. The issue lies in the fact that the corporation *expects* the latter to be true.

In addition to business and moral arguments for diversity, there is also sentiment among corporations that the growing number of women and minorities who are new entrants to the corporation will present new issues and concerns. Beyond the goal of attracting and retaining a diverse talent pool is the challenge of incorporating not only individual differences but also establishing a work environment wherein the relational aspect of diversity is achieved between the individual employee and the corporation. In this context, diversity wears the face of pluralism.

The pluralistic dimension of diversity requires corporations to institute strategies that fit with the mission and values of the corporation. It involves establishing relationships between the corporation and individual employees that focus on interdependency and mutual respect (Norton and Fox 1997). This is accomplished by an integration of cultures that is characterized by members of each retaining significant aspects of their own culture, while viewing other cultures as having qualities that are attractive (Tung 1993).

My friend Riana and I were discussing the issue of diversity in corporate America. She recalled a recent situation at her workplace a few days earlier. Her employer, a large and prestigious software corporation, decided to have an outdoor luncheon for the employees in her division. At least a hundred or so people were present. After enjoying a delicious buffet meal, Riana looked around and noticed something quite striking. Each dining table was filled with her colleagues eating and chatting about issues of the day. But the most revealing aspect of the observation was that each table represented only one racial or ethnic group. African Americans sat with African Americans. Latinos sat with Latinos. Whites sat with whites. And Asians, the largest group present, filled several tables that accommodated people of Asian descent. When not forced to interact with each other, individual groups of the same racial and ethnic background *chose* to sit together enjoying social exchanges and interactions. Although somewhat troubling to Riana, she was not surprised. Opportunities for informal connections, gatherings, and interactions usually result in individuals choosing a group with whom they are most familiar. Beverly Tatum's work *Why Are All The Black Kids Sitting Together in the Cafeteria?* proposes that adolescents and even adults participate in racial and ethnic groups of whom they are a member because of comfort, trust, and familiarity.

Groups performing formal tasks for the corporation typically mirror a mix of gender and racial and ethnic backgrounds. In most cases, sheer competence plays the most important part in assigning work projects. In a majority of information technology corporations, teams are the vehicle by which talent is shown. Thus, it is through the interaction of individuals seeking to meet their own needs and managing the needs of the corporation that they attempt to balance the nature of who they are as individuals while managing their work experiences. I would certainly agree that all other things being equal, individuals having varying kinds and degrees of interpersonal and professional relationships at work can only benefit the corporation and have value in terms of job satisfaction, commitment, self-esteem, and, even occasionally, high productivity.

A few corporations indicate that forecasts on how the U.S. workforce population is changing from one that had been traditionally male-dominated to one that includes a growing number of women and minorities have caused many companies to pause and consider the implications of such demographic change inside the workplace. In fact, such projections have motivated 12 percent of corporations to become better prepared for the diverse needs of new entrants. My work reveals that corporations implement diversity strategies to attempt to create and foster work environments that are pluralistic—that is, that are welcoming and tolerant, and that value the contributions of all employees, including white males. Interestingly, these companies are older and are considered to be diversity pioneers. They have weathered the storm of striving for and achieving diversity and now are dealing with the next level of its evolution—the integration not only of different groups, but also of individuals who represent different ideas, styles, and values. The plural support of diversity is demonstrated throughout the entire corporation. Across all business units, many corporations establish and implement diversity practices that encourage the recognition of individuality and the distinctiveness of individual employees. As Norton and Fox put it, such practices affirm differences as organizational assets to be capitalized upon as well as re-warded as desirable behaviors.

In essence, the pluralistic face of diversity allows corporations to implement strategies designed to prepare the corporation for what is inevitable—a growing number of women and minority employees. It is critical to understand that plural arguments encourage corporations to create and foster a working environment—actual physical spaces and cul-tures—in which individuals are motivated and comfortable to contribute to those activities that enable the corporation to achieve its goals and maintain its competitive advantage.

The issue of attracting and hiring women and minorities in corpora-tions cannot be simply reduced to implementing tailored strategies. The need for *justifications* continues to support corporate decisions to adopt and implement diversity practices. With the backlash against Affirmative Action, senior executives are addressing the diversity issue and many are strategizing about it. However, what is certain here is that business, moral, and plural arguments support the adoption and implementation of diversity strategies and, in turn, promote corporations' self-interests.

To sum, the business argument of diversity relies on attracting and re-taining human capital—the kind that is innovative, creative, and produc-tive, which translates into diverse products and greater profits. Framing diversity in these terms makes it easier to sell. However, corporations that use the business argument to support diversity fail to consider the contin-gency factor. As discussed in Chapter 5, my research on historically black colleges and universities (HBCUs) indicates that the implementation of diversity strategies is contingent on the economy as well as the availability and accessibility of women and minority talent. When the economy is booming, the recruitment and retention of diverse talent is easier than when the economy is sluggish. Thus, the business argument for diversity will go in and out of season—depending on the economic winds of time.

Nonetheless, the moral face of diversity is rarely influenced by busi-ness strategy but brings with it a perception of greater social legitimacy. Corporations use the face of morality as a justification for establishing and maintaining ties, mostly financial, with women and minority organi-zations. Grounded in the tenets of equality and justice for all, arguments of a moral nature lead corporations to be good corporate citizens—to do the right thing! Usually, doing the right thing has its advantages for the corporation. Winning diversity awards and recognitions, gaining public approval, and avoiding litigation are desired outcomes for any corporation. The principle of good corporate citizenship, however, tends to reflect the corporation's *external* relationships and responsibilities. When addressing diversity as an internal effort, some corporations in this study are prone to ignore the issue altogether. Others tend to rely on the idea of plurality or valuing differences as justification for adopting and implementing diversity strategies.

The pluralistic face of diversity justifies corporations' engagement in a process of integration. The task, then, is to create an environment where common and uncommon backgrounds and characteristics of individuals are not only recognized but also valued. In this context, diversity supported by plurality is not solely in the purview of the human resources departments or the CEO. Instead, its efforts are sanctioned throughout the corporation. In effect, diversity as a force for plurality is about systems *change* and *preparation* rather than individuals' attitudes and behaviors toward it. A key dimension of the pluralistic face of diversity in corporations is rewards and incentives, which are discussed in detail in the succeeding chapter.

It is in the underlying assumptions about diversity that we find social forces that drive and even constrain corporations' decisions to adopt and implement strategies to attract and retain women and minorities. Be they consumers, markets, population demographics, or social inequality, corporations interpret these forces as facilitators of enhanced business opportunities. Given this interpretation, the *societal* intent of workplace inclusion, which is predicated on fairness, respect, and equal opportunity, becomes blurred in the face of corporate self-interest. The faces of diversity are alive and well. As justifications for doing diversity, business, moral, and plural arguments give shape to the policies and practices that embody why and how corporations seek to recruit, hire, and retain women and minorities. Together, these arguments provide a foundation for establishing concrete structures and behaviors that ultimately affect the entire culture of the corporation.

Chapter Seven

Corporations are social organizations, a theater in which men and women realize or fail to realize purposeful and productive lives.

—Leslie Conway "Lester" Bangs,
American music journalist, author and musician;
writer for Creem and Rolling Stone magazines.

Chapter Seven
Getting Them and Keeping Them

Structures are in place. However, more work remains. Once the company recruits women and minority talent, how does it keep them? What must the corporation do to ensure that the resources in recruiting and hiring women and minority talent are not wasted by the revolving door syndrome? After all, women and minority science and engineering professionals are scarce. They do not come a dime a dozen. In the marketplace, they are competitive and desirable. Typical of most scientists and engineers, they enjoy rotating job assignments and even rotating companies. They are motivated by better salary offers, fringe benefits, and innovative projects. Unlike some occupations where women and minorities are reasonably represented, women and minority scientists and engineers are rarely bound to one corporation. They are capable of reinventing their skills to be highly attractive and desirable in the labor market. Thus, women and minority scientists and engineers, given the nature and specialization of changing technologies, are not bound to one corporation. As such, corporations are faced with the challenge of not only recruiting them but also securing them for the long haul. Corporations must meet their needs in order to retain them as valuable assets to the corporation.

It is no secret that getting and keeping the best and the brightest professionals is vital to the corporation's financial growth, stability, reputation, and competitive advantage. Jockeying for people to become a part of and remain in the corporation is an essential means to obtaining organizational goals. For those who carry out the day-to-day human resources functions within the corporation, getting and keeping skilled and qualified women and minority professionals rests on the favor of corporate leadership and internal decision-making. In essence, an interest in diversity on the part of corporate leaders is key to recruiting and retaining qualified professionals, but especially women and minorities. Although previous chapters have discussed the role of the external environment on the presence of diversity strategies, there exists yet another structure in which diversity behavior is played out in the corporation—that is, the role of corporate leadership.

Executive Leadership

Where the head goes, the body will follow. In most organizations, the leader sets the tone, climate, and pace. In the case of diversity, the role of leadership is considered its champion. Why is leadership a driver of the issue of diversity in American corporations? What is unique about senior-level management that can motivate or destroy a corporation's efforts to do diversity? Few research studies point to the relationship between leadership and the adoption of diversity strategies. However, a closer look at corporate leadership shows that leaders' stances on recruiting and retaining women and minorities affects employees' attitudes and perceptions of their importance to the overall corporation.

Diversity exists and survives in most corporations because of its attachment to organizational goals and strategic plans. As discussed in the previous chapter, it evolves and is usually manifested in a particular business context. The beginning of this process usually occurs with leaders. CEOs and senior-level managers have access to tools to make things happen. But despite this access, corporate leaders have been blamed for the absence of and problems associated with diversity. It is important to note that, realistically, most senior executives are faced with other pressing challenges and problems that are likely to outweigh the issue of diversity. Yet, many human resources and diversity professionals are convinced that the adoption of diversity strategies must begin at the top of the corporation.

Consider the following observation from my study. In a meeting of several CEOs of the nation's top Fortune 500 companies, diversity is the only agenda item of the day. Presentations center on projected U.S. demographics and their impact on the labor force by 2050, math and science competencies at the high school and college levels, global competition, and recommended strategies to capitalize on untapped talent. Recognizing the need for stronger ties to the nation's education system and the military, discussions yield insights into the role of the CEO and senior executives to create and push forward formal diversity strategies as a part of day-to-day operations. Having heard myriad impressive explanations and ideas for "doing diversity," a sociologist present at the meeting asked the group of the nation's corporate elites how do they plan to implement their vision of diversity in their corporations. Amidst a round of chuckles and laughter, a CEO responded by saying, "A memo, with my signature, of course, stating 'Just do it!'"

This observation is not only about the stroke of the CEO's pen and the issuing of an edict but it also identifies specifically the preference and desire of the Chief Executive Officer. Simply put, it's what the leader of the pack wants. Without great discussion, debate, or argument, from the lips of the CEO, diversity rarely requires more than assessment, modification, implementation, monitoring, and evaluation. As a CEO priority, business units are urged to establish and meet diversity goals and be satisfied with them. Seventy-six percent of corporations reached the same conclusion that the role of the CEO and senior-level managers is crucial in the adoption of diversity strategies. They agree that "it starts at the top." Without the push from the top, diversity behaviors are not a *real* part of the corporation's day-to-day business practices. However, there is some resistance at the top as well. Terri, an HR executive, commented, "The greatest challenge associated with diversity and senior-level leadership is finding a CEO who believes in diversity and who is not afraid to address its issues throughout the organization." However, if not pushed down from the top, diversity efforts are likely to spring forth from the bottom of the corporation. The social forces of diversity are too great to deny it admission into the corporation altogether.

Diversity downward rather than upward—that is, the push for diversity from the employee base poses an entirely different set of challenges and complexities. Petitions, proposals, and complaints tend to character-ize diversity from the lower tiers of the corporation. In most corporations, to see diversity downward is to have newly formed women and minority associations and task forces, to encourage participation in contentious meetings with departments such as HR and to have senior-level execu-tives, including the chairman, develop diversity measures, outcomes, and written reports. It is to engage a process from the grassroots level that tends to require much time, energy, and process, to say the least.

Corporations believe that diversity downward is based on the belief that management is ineffective and unfair. Corporate leaders tend to respond nervously to and are a bit uncomfortable with the *new* thinking about diversity. They are concerned with allegations of racism, sexism, and discriminatory labor practices. Diversity downward can challenge the integrity of senior leadership and conjures the idea of the possibility of class action suits and negative publicity. Unlike diversity behaviors emanating from the top, diversity downward assumes a lack of involve-ment from the CEO and senior executives. It implies inadequate, poor, or absent diversity-related practices.

In her interview, Terri explains this further:

> At this corporation, one of the omissions is that the diversity strategies seem to be sound and to be realistic, but the execu-tion systemically hasn't happened. I would say that compared to other companies that I know of and what they're doing, recruiting strategies are fundamental. Here, they are not as advanced or progressive as other IT companies. The commit-ment is very poor. It needs to come from the top. Hopefully with our new CEO, I am sure with her on board, things will change. But I really don't know.

The issue of accountability is raised for those corporations that report a lack of involvement from their CEO or senior executives. Accountability, in this context, refers to adhering to monitoring and evaluating diversity strategies and outcomes. In turn, there are sanctions for failing to meet the corporation's diversity goals. When diversity plans are not supported from the top *formally,* that is, they are not a part of the CEO's or senior management's priorities, diversity practices tend to be weak and often lack ambition. They wind up mirroring symbolic gestures and tend to be reduced to corporate rhetoric. Little to no accountability for diversity generates weak and ineffective diversity plans and thus poor diversity outcomes.

Many corporations argue that accountability, finally, is associated with the appointment of those responsible for the adoption and implementation of diversity strategies throughout the corporation. The CEO and senior executives appoint the diversity leader. In many cases, corporations either have separate offices responsible for diversity or minimally, they attach diversity goals to an existing office or department. Because an official and formal appointment is made, there is usually an investment in time and money toward the corporation's diversity goals. In turn, it is the case that diversity leaders are given formal mandates and are held accountable to them by senior-level management.

At the same time, 84 percent of corporations echo the necessity for leadership to be diffused throughout the corporation. In the case of adopting and implementing diversity strategies, leadership from the top down is not enough. If strategies to attract and retain women and minorities are to be successful, then leadership in this area must be dispersed throughout the entire corporation. In this view, accountability must be shared and diversity leadership should flow up and down and throughout the corporation. Walter agrees with this argument by attesting that "every business unit in this corporation is responsible for establishing and meeting diversity goals. The responsibility does not lie alone with HR. It's the only way we will become truly a diverse organization."

The visibility and actions of corporate leadership concerning diversity is likely to rest on the need to sustain balance and harmony within the corporation. Internally, corporate leaders either drive or hinder the adoption of diversity strategies. Motivated by external environmental conditions and internal constituents, the formal adoption of diversity strategies assumes accountability. Hence, accountability sounds the gavel that sustains the adoption of diversity strategies as *action*—actual behavior. Walter further contends that "without accountability in this company, no one here would take our diversity initiatives seriously. Our chairman makes it known throughout the company that each vice president and their associates must meet their diversity goals or else!"

Leadership is not a synonym for change. Although leaders can catalyze change, they can not implement policy in a vacuum. Diversity strategies that receive their signal from the top have a better chance of surviving throughout the corporation than those that do not. However, it is important to note that the activities associated with developing and implementing such strategies are done not at the top but at the lower levels of the organization. Change that results from activities is achieved over time and reflects the will of all members, not just leaders. Terri makes this point clear: "Sometimes I think the CEO and his executives have it easy; they issue the orders and the rest of us go to war. Orders without works are dead. It's like a good leader isn't very good without very good followers."

So far, most corporations assume that the CEO and senior executives have a clue about diversity and its relevance to the corporation. Yet, several companies report that they honestly believe that their corporate leadership is either "in denial about the need to address diversity" or "they don't know where to begin." In many instances, then, corporations run the risk of doing business as usual—that is, recruiting and hiring those who are familiar, comfortable, and in-network—in short, all white males. Sandra expounds on this point:

> At a corporate-wide event, senior management was up front and staged before everyone. They were all white men! I wondered if anyone else caught this. Are the senior executives *aware* of this? Later, I asked my senior vice president if he thought this was okay. He looked at me with a blank stare—totally clueless. He asked me, what do you mean by this?

Here opportunity, information, and exposure are crucial. Assumptions about the CEO's interest in, and knowledge and understanding of diversity are key factors. Being aware of and understanding the organizational features that impact human behavior and motivation is essential in the modern corporation. This leads to a better quality of work life and more equitable opportunities for all employees. Although corporate leaders are instrumental in influencing the adoption of diversity strategies, there are also other means by which people use the corporation and operate through it that contribute to the adoption of diversity strategies. These involve the presence of minority human resources mangers and women and minority employees.

Research on a number of professional groups—nurses, physicians, lawyers, human resources mangers, social workers, accountants, teachers, stockbrokers, librarians, engineers, and advertising account executives—indicates that there is a relationship between professionalization and bureaucratization. In short, the attitudes and values associated with one's profession may interface with the organization's values and rules. However, research evidence in this area suggests that there is conflict between the professional and the organization. Richard Hall's work informs us that this conflict is not inevitable and should not be assumed without demonstration. For example, legal departments within large organizations are not necessarily more bureaucratized than law firms of comparable size. Lawyers working in a trust department in a bank may be working in an organization that is similar or perhaps identical to the one they would find in a law firm. Thus, these findings suggest that there are organizational structures that are quite comparable to the degree of professionalization of its members.

Professionalization

When professionals become employees of an organization, they bring with them their standards, rules of conduct, and values—simply put, their interests. There is a recent body of research that describes the influence of professionals in organizations as *agents of diffusion*. Specifically, this research suggests that groups' professional interests guide, shape, and determine corporate responses. The works of Edelman et al. (1992), Kelly and Dobbin (1999), and Sutton and Dobbin (1996) find that professional groups such as lawyers and human resources managers turn legal ambiguity into a professional and organizational asset. They exaggerate the *risk* of litigation in order to win corporate resources by lobbying executives to create and fund what they want—specialized personnel systems. Similarly, Kelly and Dobbin discovered that having a professional within the organization to advocate for the adoption of maternity leave policy leads to formalized personnel functions that impact the organization's recruitment, hiring, training, and retention efforts.

In this study, multivariate analyses indicate that the presence of women and minority human resources professionals is associated with the adoption of diversity strategies. Their presence is important and not coincidental. Women and minority human resources professionals with managerial responsibility for recruiting and retaining women and minorities are a visible symbol or token representation of the corporation's commitment to addressing diversity. Corporations with a high-level commitment to diversity are more likely to choose diversity leaders who represent women and diverse racial and ethnic groups. Several corporations contend that this fosters a sense of trust and familiarity among prospective employees. Women and minority job candidates view the corporation more favorably if ushered in by those they identify with.

My analysis of the influence of women and minority human resources professionals is sustained advocacy. Given their vested professional and personal interest in meeting the corporation's diversity goals, it is likely that these groups understand the organizational politics that drive and restrain progress in recruiting and retaining women and minorities. In her interview, Linda, a human resources director, put it this way:

> I've been with this company nearly 27 years and I know where many of the bones are buried. I am pretty successful in recruiting diverse employees, too. The directors respect what I do and I am sure that I make a difference here. I work hard at it, though. Just look around—many of these people of color were recruited by me!

Trust

The issue of trust is paramount. Racist and sexist attitudes and ideologies are alive and well in the American workplace. These attitudes diminish trust in situations where recruitment and hiring takes place. When discussing her feelings about white males recruiting for diversity, Constance, a minority human resources executive, states, "I don't trust them as far as

I can throw them! They say they are concerned about diversity but only recruit at Virginia Tech and MIT. What about Howard University and Florida A&M?" There is a general consensus about most corporations that when it comes down to diversity issues, women and minority human resources professionals are considered a safer bet than their white male counterparts.

Because gender and race are the most visible, significant, and longstanding of all diversity indicators, women and minority human resources managers rank them among the top issues concerning workplace inclusion. As opposed to age, disability, sexual orientation, and national origin, there is a conscious effort to keep gender and race at the forefront in their diversity plans. In a profession-driven industry like information technology, the issues of race and gender continue to raise their heads given the underrepresentation of U.S.-born women and minorities in the information technology sector. This sentiment is expressed by Sandra in her interview in the following way:

> In information technology, it is sometimes very difficult to find women and minorities with the education and work experience we're looking for. So, our efforts are focused on ensuring that over time we have these groups represented more equitably in the company. We do care about people with disabilities and gay individuals, but we are still struggling to recruit successfully females and minorities, especially and in general."

Personal and Professional Obligation

Personal and professional obligation drives women and minority human resources professionals to place an emphasis on recruiting and retaining females and minorities. They identify with and are sympathetic to the "racialized" and "gendered" workplace experiences. They want to do all that is legally and ethically possible to ensure that these groups get their fair share. In fact, over half of corporations report that women and minority human resources managers use their positions to launch diversity programs in significant ways. They hire consultants to develop and implement diversity plans. They secure funds to create affinity groups.

They implement executive leadership and formal mentoring programs and they manage to have audiences with the CEO. Communications efforts are used to spread the corporation's intentions toward diversity inside and outside the organization.

Eighty percent of corporations indicate that women and minority human resources professionals feel as though their positions require and obligate them to be aggressive in recruiting and retaining women and minority talent. They use their professional training and knowledge to skillfully influence key players in the corporation to pursue with rigor diversity plans and initiatives. According to Walter's interview:

> After attending the national conferences on diversity each year, I schedule meetings with the senior vice president to discuss those key issues we should be addressing; my association meetings are very helpful in helping the corporation define its major priorities around diversity.

Decision-Making

The presence of a female or minority human resources manager is crucial to decision-making inside the corporation. Simply being present and participatory during meetings, for example, makes a difference. Nearly 73 percent of corporations report that the presence of women and minority human resources managers at meetings often changes the course of action regarding recruiting and hiring decisions. When asked about the possibility of women and minority human resources managers not being present, corporations expressed uncertainty about decisions and their impact on recruiting and hiring. Constance shared this experience in her interview:

> Until the faces in the room change, in the decision making conference room, the boardroom—and it happens at all levels in a corporation; it's not just always the board—that's when true change happens. I'll give you an example. I was working here in this business as the HR director, and so I had the whole business HR function to manage. And I was getting ready to

move on to a new role, and the general manager at the time was looking to hire a new program management director, and we had two candidates: We had a female candidate and a white male candidate. Unfortunately, the general manager's staff at that time was all male with the exception of me. And he knew that I was moving on and he wanted my opinion on these two candidates, and I said, "Well, I think they're equally qualified candidates. They both have their individual strengths that I think balance out which one is the better candidate. So think about this one thing. When I leave your staff you're going to look around the room and you're going to see only male faces. So in this decision, think about that. If you hire the male you will look around the room and continue to only see all male faces. If you hire the female, you will at least have a different perspective brought to the party." And that's what I call a moment of truth. That's when that manager, depending on their value system and whether or not they think that's important or not, makes the right or wrong decision, or makes at least *a* decision, call it what you want. In this case he decided to hire the woman. They were equally qualified, and she brought them something to the party that the other guy couldn't bring and that was a female perspective. And that's what changes, incrementally changes, things over time.

A Critical Mass

Yet at the same time, evidence suggests that diversity strategies are associated with the mere *presence* of women and minority employees and not exclusively women and minority human resources professionals; the greater the proportion of women and minority employees—that is, African Americans, Hispanic Americans, and Native Americans—the more likely the presence of diversity strategies. As for Asian Americans, compared to all other minority groups, diversity strategies are not consequential given their overrepresentation in the information technology sector.

Sociologist Rosabeth Moss Kanter, in *Men and Women of the Corporation,* examines the impact of the relative numbers of women and minorities in the corporation. She describes how the increase of the number of women and minorities affects the level of hostility and stereotyping toward them. Kanter concludes that negative attitudes and behaviors decrease as the number of women and minorities in the corporation increase.

As found in this study, nearly 90 percent of corporations agree that there is a link between the proportion of women and minority employees and the adoption of diversity strategies. They conclude that the presence *alone* of women and minorities throughout the corporation encourages not only corporate diversity structures and behaviors but also increases the attractiveness of the corporation to women and minority job candidates. Reporting on this finding is one interviewee, Tammy, a human resources senior manager with the following observation:

> I think the main thing is people want to come to the corporation and see, especially at the top, people that look like them, so they know they can make it too. So women want to see women in senior leadership executive ranks, and women minorities especially. As you know, there's a lot fewer women minority executives, there's a lot more minority male executives, so people want to see people at the top that look like them. So if they come and they're a minority female and they don't see any minority females at the senior leader executive ranks or even throughout the corporation in general, they may be reluctant to come and work for the company. They may still come, but they may not stay because they may think no one here looks like me. But I think that's really the key—our companies promoting women and minorities higher than just middle management level.

There is strength in numbers. A critical mass of women and minorities has its privileges. The more women and minorities, the more opportunities for advancement. In fact, a greater proportion of these groups allow diversity initiatives to go beyond the monitoring of numerical representation to tackling those gender and racial and ethnic issues that constrain the corporation—for example, structural barriers such as promotions, salaries, job assignments, and executive leadership opportunities. As suggested by Kanter, the lives of women and minorities in the corporation are influenced by the proportion in which they find themselves. Significant proportions of women and minorities produce internal strong support groups, social and professional relationships and interactions, shared experiences, acceptance, and familiarity. When women and minorities find corporations that meet these characteristics, they remain with them.

On the other hand, the scarcity of women and minorities is less likely associated with the adoption of diversity strategies. When women and minorities are absent, the perception of the corporation is "too white" and "too male." Often, in situations where the corporation is too white and too male, the scarce number of women and minorities are considered *tokens*. During her interview, Jillian, a junior human resources manager, provides an interesting example of the relationship between the small proportion of women and minorities and the absence of diversity strategies:

> At this company, we don't have formal policies or procedures concerning diversity. Our CEO feels as though we don't need it. He always says that we are not a racist organization. We practice equal opportunity. But, we only have 21 minorities out of 644 employees. And two of them are associate vice presidents. They're known as our tokens. If we could do more with diversity, then I am sure that our numbers would increase and we'd have more minority senior managers, too.

In coming to understand women and minorities as gatekeepers in the corporation, there are a couple of concepts that should be taken into account. First, there is indication that diversity strategies rely on the involvement of women and minority human resources professionals. There is pause for some concern here. Although it is easy to get hooked on the idea that women and minorities as gatekeepers is advantageous to the recruitment and retention of women and minorities, there is no guarantee that anyone will get or keep a job. Thus, the presence of these professionals is not a "magic bullet" for bringing women and minorities into the corporation.

Stereotypes

Forty-three percent of corporations report that certain diversity activities geared toward the recruitment and retention of women and minorities may hinder full acceptance and equality from their white counterparts. Some activities reinforce stereotypes about women's and minorities' need for "extra" or "special" conditions before they are fit to compete in corporate America. As gatekeepers, the role of women and minority human resources professionals includes that of *informant*. However, this role is potentially problematic. Genuinely concerned about the welfare of new hires, these informants intentionally shape the perceptions and future experiences of new hires. They provide them with the lay of the land. They issue cautions and warnings. New hires are likely to take this information at face value and act accordingly. The danger of this is limited or nonexistent interactions and work relationships that could be pivotal to an individual's advancement in the corporation. On the contrary, having a stake in the successful adoption and implementation of diversity strategies, women and minority human resources professionals provide access to organizational structures for certain groups who are the most likely excluded. In essence, they make diversity a reality.

The critical mass of women and minorities in the corporation is an ideal situation. It allows the organization to balance itself in a way that takes advantage of its primary resources—people. The presence of more women and more minorities draws more women and minorities. Hence, the link between the adoption of diversity strategies and a greater proportion of these groups is an indication that the strategies are effective. Over time, the corporation is likely to become tolerant of differences and moves to a place wherein differences become human capital and thus a valuable resource—human talent. All of these factors—the role of leadership and women and minorities as gatekeepers—represent the ways in which diversity strategies are constituted and become a part of corporate practices to bring in and keep women and minorities. However, there are other mechanisms for attracting and retaining them. These mechanisms are rooted in what researchers call bureaucratic control practices.

Hiring and Retention Practices

How does the corporation attract the best and brightest women and minority professionals? How do they encourage and motivate them to do their best work? How do they gain their loyalty and minimize their voluntary departures? Is it by promising career advancements, support, training, and extrinsic incentives? Having competed successfully for them, most corporations prefer to *keep* women and minorities on board rather than function as a revolving door. As corporations adopt and implement diversity strategies, they invent practices that affect employee behavior. These practices are fundamental because they establish the structural conditions or structural *controls* that shape the work experiences of women and minorities. In turn, organizational arrangements become just as consequential to controlling employee behavior as to generating profits.

In the classic work *Contested Terrain,* Richard Edwards (1979, 20) argues that corporations develop formalized methods of "structural" control. He maintains that there are two possibilities of how this structural control shows up in corporations: "1) More formal, consciously contrived controls could be embedded in the physical structure of the labor process (producing "technical" control) or 2) in its social structure (producing bureaucratic control)." Edwards suggests that over a period of time, corporations require both technical and bureaucratic control given that new systems enable control to become more "institutional" and less obvious to employees. In fact, both technical and bureaucratic control provide a means for the corporation to control what Edwards terms "intermediate layers"—the lines that extend supervision and power.

Bureaucratic Control

As a method of controlling workers, technical control refers to the notion of the machinery itself directing the labor process and establishing the pace of work. In contrast, bureaucratic control focuses on the formalization and implementation of rules and procedures within the corporation. Bureaucratic control rests on the assumption that control is embedded in the social structure or the social relations of the work environment. The defining feature of bureaucratic control is the institutionalization of hierarchical power—rules of law—the firm's law—replacing rules by supervisorial command in terms of work functions, evaluation of performance, execution of sanctions and rewards, and managers and workers alike becoming subject to dictates of company policy. Moreover, under the tenets of bureaucratic control, work becomes highly stratified, each job has its own title and description and impersonal rules determine promotion.

As many theorists have pointed out, the notion of bureaucratic control as a method of institutionalizing *positive* incentives is quite important. Simply put, proper behavior within the corporation is rewarded. Further, positive incentives tend to heighten an employee's sense of personal growth or career mobility that lies in front of them *within the firm*. In accordance with the general logic of bureaucratic control, Edwards informs us that reprimand, suspension, dismissal, and other punishments become penalties for specialized categories of offenses. In this case, punishments flow from the established organizational rules and procedures.

Monitoring and Evaluation

Bureaucratic control practices are alive and well in this study. As shown in Table 7.1, I conduct multivariate analyses and results indicate that some corporations' hiring behaviors are targeted toward women and minorities. These findings reveal an important characteristic of diversity strategies—the *monitoring* and *evaluation* of hiring practices geared toward women and minorities. Corporations that are serious about establishing and meeting diversity goals are usually *required* by senior management to implement supervision to ensure that hiring objectives are met and, if they are not, the question of why not must be answered. Monitoring and evaluating the hiring procedures for women and minorities is quite familiar to most corporations. The influence of federal mandates rings a bell here. As discussed in Chapter 4, federal mandates such as Equal Employment Opportunity and Affirmative Action programs are

Table 7.1
Logistic Estimates for Corporations' Hiring Activities for Women and
Minorities on Adoption of Diversity Strategies

Additional Variable	Firm Size B(SE)	Firm Age B(SE)	Firm Revenue B(SE)	Additional Variable B(SE)	Model X²	Pseudo R²	Sample Size
Monitor/Evaluate Hiring Strategies	.132(.377)	.359(.386)	.228(.206)	.556(.502)	8.415ᴬ	.099	81
Offer Special Hiring Incentives (bonuses, fringes)	.111(.374)	.230(.385)	.249(.203)	.282(.731)	5.673	.068	80
Provide On-the-Job Training to New Hires	.109(.375)	.235(.381)	.280(.199)	.780(.916)	7.503	.088	81
Rely on Colleges/Universities for Training	.256(.365)	.328(.383)	.242(.196)	-.485(.527)	7.956ᴬ	.091	83
Contract Externally for Training of New Hires	.184(.336)	.300(.379)	.269(.204)	.457(.614)	7.660ᴬ	.088	83
Majority of Women/Minorities Needing Training	.090(.371)	.490(.409)	.237(.199)	.620(.528)	8.002ᴬ	.095	80

ᴬSignificant at the $p < .10$.

associated with the presence of diversity strategies. In this case, the monitoring and evaluation of hiring practices for women and minorities tends to suggest the influence of government mandates.

Incentives and On-the-Job Training

Positive incentives also have their place in the corporation. My survey data in Table 7.1 also reveal that offering special incentives and providing on-the-job training characterize the hiring practices for women and minorities. Corporations that implement diversity strategies report that women and minority new hires are often persuaded to join their company because of attractive signing bonuses, competitive salaries, and fringe benefits. Given the demand for women and minority professionals in the information technology sector, hiring practices are likely to employ positive and generous incentives, often financial, to attract these groups. And, these incentives are legitimized through and in the corporation's formal diversity strategies.

Corporation's Reputation

Not all incentives are visible or tangible. In fact, the most important means of bringing in women and minority new hires is invisible. In many cases, women and minority new hires are drawn to the corporation because of the firm's reputation for hiring, promoting, and retaining them. There are always lists of "Top 100," "Top 50," and "Top 10 Best Corporations for Women or Minorities." Issued by national organizations or special groups, their mission is to protect the professional interests and direct the professional experiences of women and minorities in corporate America. In recent years, national organizations have come up with a "Best Diversity Employer" award to recognize those corporations that promote and advance diverse populations in the workplace. There are also lists generated by national groups that identify corporations that are the *worst* employers for women and minorities.

These listings usually present themselves as rankings. They are indeed influential, believable, and likely to contribute to a corporation's success or difficulty in hiring diverse populations. The role of print media especially in informing the public and prospective employees about the opportunity structures, climate of the organization, and recent experiences of former and current employees is quite powerful. Corporations agree that a firm's reputation is essential to attracting women and minority professionals. Sandra states in her interview:

> I think a corporation's reputation is the best way to recruit and retain females and minorities. Most corporations are looked at just the way you look at colleges. What does a corporation have for me that is going to help me with my career?"

The Retention of Women and Minorities

Successfully hiring a female or minority does not necessarily mean retaining them. Often, many women and minority professionals move around and rarely do they stay with a firm for the life of their career. They seek out and accept job opportunities with other firms that allow for greater advancement, higher pay, and more interesting work assignments. For those women and minorities fresh out of college, it is almost expected that they will not remain with the corporation for more than five to seven years before moving on to greater heights in the industry. Similar to entering a college or university, these groups master a great deal of knowledge and develop exceptional skills sets and look forward to senior-level technical or administrative positions with a competing firm. This revolving door syndrome may prove somewhat challenging for corporations who wish to retain talented women and minorities.

However, some corporations have mixed feelings about the responsibility of retaining women and minorities. In fact, 64 percent of corporations do not view it as a responsibility at all. There is no relationship between hiring the best and the brightest *and* retaining them. In most cases, white male senior managers and executives may not perceive that there is a retention problem in the company. Usually their perception of retention problems is driven by numerical indicators, which typically results in problems associated with employee turnover rates. Many corporations conclude that the link between hiring and retaining women and minority talent is too often based on perception. Consequently, this perception tends to impact hiring practices to attract the best and the brightest women and minority talent.

However, corporations that are concerned with encouraging women and minority groups to remain with them are less fixated on numerical goals. They tend to implement a range of retention activities that are diffused throughout the corporation. The retention activities are always a function of the corporation's formal diversity strategies. They range from activities such as offering executive leadership training and rotating job assignments and lateral assignments, to implementing succession plans, offering mentoring programs and support groups, to providing job training for specific job assignments, and implementing employee-recognition programs, to publishing internal newsletters and publications for women and minority groups (see Table 7.2).

Retention Activities

As shown in Table 7.3, I take a closer look at these activities under multivariate analyses. My findings indicate that there are five activities most significantly related to retaining women and minorities, presented in order of importance. First, executive leadership training is the corporation's first step in endorsing women and minorities as potential leaders. This training provides curricula developed to address the varying challenges and opportunities inherent across every level of senior management. As a retention practice, it offers an opportunity for promotion—to ultimately become a senior executive with all rights and privileges. In many corporations with diversity strategies, women and minorities are selected for executive leadership training. They are the talent who have begun a journey wherein the corporation nurtures their progress. They have demonstrated high achievement and are on their way to a membership in a select and elite group—executive-level management in a Fortune 500 corporation. This is perhaps the pinnacle of one's career in corporate America—to make it to the top. Any realistic opportunity to achieve this goal—with the help of the corporation—is reason to stay with them. Career mobility is what keeps women and minorities with their employers.

Second, in a profession like information technology, rotating job assignments is an important means of retaining women and minority

They legitimize not only the work experiences of women and minority professionals but also their presence through a formal written means of communication within the corporation. At the same time, newsletters and publications are a preferred mechanism for translating the corporation's commitment to diversity as well as other important issues.

Retention practices that are linked to diversity strategies are *not* based on reward, recognition, or even evaluation. Rather, these practices have to do with *performance.* In general, retaining women and minorities in the corporation is simply a matter of making sure that there are opportunities for career advancement, intellectual stimulation, and professional growth and development. In order for this to occur, the corporation is faced with the daunting challenge of creating and maintaining a work environment that is accepting and welcoming. It must perpetuate trust and demonstrate an ethic of caring.

Despite corporations' efforts to implement certain practices and activities designed to retain women and minority talent, there are other challenges and difficulties that are more volatile for women and minorities and the corporation. For many women and minority professionals, their decision to remain with a company hinges on the strength of their work relationship with their supervisor. For those driven by career advancement and professional development opportunities, it is no secret that this process begins with one's boss.

The supervisor–subordinate relationship is shaped and influenced by many relationship factors—for example, decisions, conflict, consensus, trust, training, support, company priorities, power, politics, evaluation, feedback, compensation, race, gender, sexual orientation assumptions, expectations, work assignments, and perceptions, to name just a few. In many supervisor–subordinate relationships, race and gender issues are known to present difficult challenges to manage and overcome. In turn, these difficult challenges are likely to impede one's career mobility and block opportunities for professional growth and development throughout the entire corporation. Yvonne shares her experiences on this matter during her interview:

> We did a retention development and advancement survey a
> couple of years ago. One thing that came out was, whom the

person works for is important—it is very important that the leader provides women and minorities opportunities, support, develops assignments and provides work that helps one grow. I think that is very key—who you work for. Everyone is working for someone, even if you're at the top. Also important is the question of am I being compensated fairly for what I'm doing? As a woman or minority, am I being paid the same for doing the same job as my white male counterpart?

The retention of women poses its own unique challenges for most corporations. Seventy-three percent of corporations report that they are faced with the problem of women leaving the company at a faster rate than any other group. They are realizing that women not only have a job in the workplace but also in the home. Assuming the domestic and traditional roles of mother and wife, many women struggle to lead balanced lives in corporate America. However, in order to encourage work/life balance, corporations are instituting work/life policies that are based on flexibility and telecommuting that help retain women professionals.

A few corporations are beginning to create career mobility policies that take into account nontraditional approaches to performing and managing work assignments. Without such accommodations, many highly performing women are being forced to leave the firm. Creating and living a well-rounded life that does not involve competing demands and priorities is the real issue for most women professionals. Several corporations are beginning to realize that developing oneself outside the firm only adds to one's value inside. However, their structures and behaviors have yet to fully reflect this realization.

As intimated by many corporations, the retention of women and minority professionals is indeed difficult. There are times when it seems as if no traditional strategy will work. They leave the corporation regardless of career opportunities, competitive salaries, or extraordinary mentoring. It is at this point that a handful of corporations point to nontraditional retention approaches that involve much creativity.

There are times when the geographic location of the corporation poses a challenge for minority employees. When the corporation is located in areas that do not have well-established African American, Latino, or

Asian communities, it may be very difficult for individuals to adapt and feel comfortable. Quality-of-life issues such as racialized preferences and tastes in food, churches, hair salons, entertainment, and community networks are often essential to leading a balanced and happy life. One interviewee, Monica, addresses this problem by offering a creative solution:

> I've always said that when you bring particularly African Americans out here in the West, one of the things that you have to look at is whether their experiences are going to be different from their place of origin. So one of the things that I advocated for, which was of course readily turned down, was to have a little retention kit—that is, probably their significant others, parents and all are going to be someplace else, so you give them a little long-distance card and you fill it up with free minutes, you know, so they can talk and call or whatever; it helps, and a couple of airplane tickets a year and other things as well just to, like, we acknowledge what you're doing.
>
> You're being an astronaut [...] you're going out to a place that you'll probably be the only one there and we acknowledge that, so here's just a little kit for you to help you with your transition. And there are other things as well that you can do, have a little guide as far as hair products or particular foods that one might like, places we know that have a good barber or a place that can do hair. It's a little transition kit. That's what makes you recruit or retain; it's the experiences that people go through.

Corporate internal factors such as employee payoffs and economic hardships pose the greatest threat to retaining women and minorities. Often, under these conditions, retention practices focused on these groups are at high risk for elimination. For example, support groups are the first to be suspended. Although most corporations strive to retain their top women and minority performers, a downturn in the economy makes it quite difficult to do so. In turn, these groups typically have no place to go either. Competitor firms are generally not hiring.

The greatest challenge for corporations in the next few decades is the successful recruitment and retention of top-performing women and minorities. Corporate leadership, women and minority gatekeepers, and hiring and retention practices geared toward women and minorities work best together to get and keep the highly qualified talent. But there are other realizations that ought to be taken into consideration. Women and minority professionals, similar to their male and white counterparts, have lives outside of the corporation. They are motivated by family, friends, spirituality, politics, community service, personal relationships, and a cadre of values and beliefs that emanate from outside the corporation. They have passion for their profession *and* their life.

If corporations want to capitalize on the extraordinary talents of women and minority professionals, they must develop diversity strategies that are totally inclusive of the varying dimensions of who they fully are. Otherwise, corporations will continue to experience the revolving-door syndrome. Likewise, women and minority professionals will continue to roam from corporation to corporation seeking a sense of belonging and the appropriate fit.

Chapter Eight

The corporation is not a person and it does not live. It is a lifeless bundle of legally protected financial rights and relationships brilliantly designed to serve money and its imperatives. It is money that flows in its veins, not blood.

—David Korten, American economist,
author, political activist and prominent critic;
former professor, Harvard Graduate School of Business

Chapter Eight
The Imperatives of Diversity

Resource dependency arguments bring information technology corporations and their strategic efforts to recruit, hire, and retain women and minorities into the center of my study's analysis. In essence, organizations, like information technology businesses, depend on their ability to control and solve external and internal resource dependencies. In the case of information technology corporations' attempts to attract, develop, and retain women and minority talent, this ability is dependent on the firm's link to the outside world. In this effort, corporations must interact with other organizations given the critical need for human resources. Hence, the *environment* is thus the critical factor in which corporations become dependent on human talent.

Considerable attention has been devoted to understanding organizational structures and behaviors and their responses to the environment in terms of resource dependencies. Grounded in theoretical arguments such as institutionalism, interorganizational relations, neoinstitutionalism, and bureaucratic control, my research provides evidence of what I consider to be four imperatives underlying the structures and behaviors of diversity: (1) *enforcement imperative,* (2) *moral imperative,* (3) *business imperative,* and (4) *pluralistic imperative.* The multiple and distinctive imperatives determine, at least in part, whether or not and to what extent corporations adopt and implement diversity strategies. I contend that these imperatives reflect corporations' justifications for adopting and implementing diversity strategies and their longstanding involvement in addressing discrimination and inequality.

The Enforcement Imperative

The enforcement imperative of diversity calls for corporations to develop and implement strategies focused on reducing risk and uncertainty associated with grievances, complaints, and lawsuits that demonstrate vulnerability to legal sanctions. In this context, diversity as enforcement *responds to* and *recognizes* situations in need of repair—that discrimination in the recruiting, hiring, and retention of women and minorities in the corporation must be eradicated in order to preempt complaints. Hence, as posed by institutional theory, federal policies such as Equal Employment Opportunity and Affirmative Action encourage corporations to adopt and institute structural defenses. This is evidenced by corporations' formal, written statements of strategies to recruit, hire, and retain women and minorities.

The enforcement imperative also dictates that corporations continue to struggle in the hiring, promotion, and retention of underrepresented groups. Affirmative Action, along with other civil rights legislation, remains crucial in aiding and prompting corporations to recognize and develop untapped and underrepresented talent. But most work organizations are not there yet. In fact, corporations that adopted diversity strategies early on did so as part of their Affirmative Action plans. Without mandates to *ensure* the development of a plan focused on hiring and retaining women and minorities, corporations would probably experience *greater* difficulty hiring and promoting women and minorities. Diversity strategies have utility in the workplace given its ties to Equal Employment Opportunity and Affirmative Action.

Lastly, the enforcement imperative encourages corporations to *physically* locate diversity offices, managers, and staff in legal departments that include Equal Employment Opportunity and Affirmative Action personnel. The structural strategy to physically align diversity personnel to corporations' legal departments demonstrates how recruiting and retention strategies focused on women and minorities are linked directly to the need to have internal proportional racial and gender balances in the workplace.

In most cases, corporations use Equal Employment Opportunity and Affirmative Action as part of a strategy to investigate the organization and *identify* diversity issues most pertinent to the recruitment and retention of women and minorities. Because most corporations continue to deal with workplace discrimination, to abandon Affirmative Action structures that tend to characterize diversity strategies would be hazardous to the corporation. What is discovered here is that Equal Employment Opportunity and Affirmative Action are foundational to the practices that underlie diversity strategies. Hence, the strategic linkage between Affirmative Action and diversity as *enforcement* is one way of responding to legal mandates and political pressures to increase the proportional representation of women and minorities. Put another way, the enforcement imperative of diversity is based on the *conception* of the liberal principle of equal opportunities—the idea of fair procedures implemented through the bureaucratization of decision-making. What is primary here is effective positive action, and the aim is to generate the perception that justice has been done. More radically, the enforcement imperative relies on the principle of the fair distribution of rewards implemented by politicization of decision-making. Effectiveness here is positive discrimination that gives preferential treatment to underrepresented groups. Here the aim is to raise consciousness so that corporations' employees take opportunities to advance the position of disadvantaged groups. For example, a corporation interviews two equally qualified candidates; selectors would choose an individual from an underrepresented group, if possible.

Lastly, diversity as an enforcer of equal opportunity addresses a climate in which many white Americans have turned against a strategy that emphasizes programs they perceive as benefiting only racial minorities. Moreover, diversity as enforcer creates an enormous impression that federal antidiscrimination efforts have largely failed and have certainly overlooked the tremendous and complicated changes in demographics that have been unfolding since the mid-1960s. In essence, diversity as enforcement of equality and justice demonstrates that politically, federal legislation is not enough to address major demographic and workplace change. For corporations, diversity as enforcement keeps the company at least one step ahead of the negative consequences of government regulations and legal mandates. It provides the corporation with a broader understanding for dealing with not only historical sexism and racism but also a contemporary perspective of corporate–employee relations that cannot be addressed by gender or race-based legislative policies or programs.

The Moral Imperative

Moral and ethical responses to workplace discrimination are generally aimed at achieving equal opportunity for women and minorities. Moreover, moral responses attempt to foster improved and better work relations and environments through tolerance, acceptance, understanding, and sensitivity to individual and group differences. The moral imperative of diversity encourages corporations to institute a strategy to recruit and retain women and minority talent because of an organizational assurance and belief that everyone should have equal opportunities. U.S. work organizations continuously attempt to correct injustices endured by women and minorities in the past. In this study, many corporations' diversity strategies are inspired by and premised on moral and ethical motives—it is simply "the right thing to do."

As mentioned earlier, an important dimension of the moral imperative encourages corporations to assume and demonstrate *social responsibility*—to be good corporate citizens. The notion of social responsibility has been met with controversy because of its business points. Some theorists claim that the corporation's overall goal is to act on behalf of its owners—its shareholders. Many would agree that corporate shareholders can certainly donate their own assets to charities that promote causes they believe in. However, in the case of the corporation, social responsibility suggests that companies are "responsible" for creating quality products and marketing them in an ethical manner in compliance with laws and regulations and with financials represented in an honest, transparent way to shareholders. But the notion that the corporation should apply its assets for social purposes, rather than for the profits of its owners, is irresponsible (Atkins 2006).

Nobel Laureate Economist Milton Friedman argues that the corporation's only social responsibility is to make profits. He claims further that social issues are in the realm of public policy, for example, government action; corporate managers have no constituency to whom they are responsible and they are not trained to make public policy decisions. Other arguments against corporate social responsibility are that it restricts the free market goal of profit maximization, it dilutes the primary goal of business, and it limits the ability to compete in a global marketplace.

Conversely, many critics of the American corporation posit that corporations have little concern for the consumer. They care nothing about the deteriorating social order and have little to no concept of ethical practices and behaviors. They are indifferent to the problems of women, minorities, and the environment. From this perspective, many scholars argue that corporations, indeed, have a responsibility to not only their shareholder, but also to society. Rousseau's *Social Contract* suggests that corporations as citizen societies have a responsibility to give back to that society in fair measure to what they receive from that society. Other arguments for corporate social responsibility claim that companies must address social issues they may have caused and should help to resolve them. Further, corporate social responsibility limits government intervention and protects corporations' self-interest. And in many ways, corporate social responsibility addresses social issues by being proactive rather than reactive.

Most theorists agree that corporate social responsibility, in part, requires the individual to consider his or her actions in terms of a whole social system and holds them responsible for the effects of actions anywhere in that system. The impact of a company's actions on society is the focus. In particular, the corporation's *performance* of social responsibility encompasses economic, legal, ethical, and discretionary or philanthropic expectations that society has of corporations at a given point in time.

One way in which corporations demonstrate social responsibility is to establish interorganizational ties within their industries. One of the assumptions underlying interorganizationalists' arguments is that interorganizational relationships exist to achieve legitimacy and public approval. In this case, corporations seek to maintain ties with women and minority organizations such as historically black colleges and universities

(HBCUs) and women and minority science and engineering professional associations.

In general, the moral imperative drives corporations to establish defined relationships with HBCUs. In most cases, they perceive themselves as financial aides to HBCUs rather than participants in substantive relationships focused on recruiting and hiring women and minority students. Hence, ties to certain HBCUs become one-sided—benefiting the HBCU. The case for women and minority science and engineering professional associations is similar. In corporations, the nature of the relationship with women and minority science and engineering associations is, again, one of dependence for financial contributions.

The moral imperative of diversity encourages corporations to assume the role of good corporate citizen through their relationships with women and minority organizations. Ethical as well as economic considerations of these groups have resulted in significant philanthropic performance on the part of the corporation. The moral imperative, layered with economic, legal, and political factors, leads corporations to develop and engage in practices such as community outreach, corporate giving, and the creation of special programs, both internal and external, that focus on the needs and conditions of women and minorities.

Interorganizational ties with women and minority organizations, especially, help corporations push their moral motives to institute diversity strategies forward. While the relationship between corporations and women and minority organizations is strained, companies still need to find ways to perform their roles as good corporate citizens, especially among vulnerable and highly visible groups. However, when ties to women and minority organizations become distinguished by ineffective behaviors, corporations make alternative choices—they choose to shift the focus from their relationships with women and minority organizations to predominantly white colleges and universities and personal networks in order to enact diversity behaviors more effectively. As argued by resource dependency theory, corporations constantly seek to manage control over critical resources by altering their choices and manipulating their environments. A moral imperative, then, makes it easier to do so and positions the corporation in a view that is publicly favorable.

The Business Imperative

An organization's ability to control external resources (or generate profits) depends on its specialized knowledge. Here, in a profession-driven business like information technology, the business imperative of diversity hinges on the acquisition of attracting, developing, and retaining human capital. Capitalizing on the hiring and retention of women and minorities contributes to corporations' business objectives. It is an approach to doing business that is aligned with a multitude of organizational business strategies, not just one or two. There is a repeated theme for most corporations—diversity makes good business sense. It is one of the corporation's best features. Supporting the assumption of external control by Pfeffer and Salancik, many corporations link diversity to the firm's business strategies in response to two environmental forces: customers and markets *and* competitive advantage and innovation.

Corporations emphasize that an increasingly diverse customer base encourages the adoption of diversity strategies. The marketing, services, and sales of information technology products that reflect the preferences of individuals' needs, wants, and styles are influential in sustaining customers. Taking advantage of the changing demographic composition of the workforce, such as the increased employment of women and minorities, is key here. This argument is founded on the belief that only corporations that attract and retain a diverse population of employees will be successful, particularly in tight labor markets. Many American corporations are persuaded by this argument. They express certainty concerning the increased buying power and financial mobility of women and minority groups. Employing groups that mirror emerging and lucrative markets makes it easier for companies to gain access to them.

Put another way, by recruiting, hiring, and retaining women and minorities, corporations increase their business opportunities—their potential to enhance their marketing strategies by capitalizing on the intellectual, creative, and technical insights and ideas of talented women and minorities. Selling goods and services is now predicated on a reasonably adequate representative workforce. In this case, corporations need the skills of women and minority professionals to enhance products and permeate diverse markets. Instituting strategies to attract and retain women and minorities provides a broader, richer, and more productive environment. The intention and desired outcome is for innovation, which translates into increased profits and performance.

Competitive advantage for most corporations means that companies must acquire the ability and capacity to create and apply new technologies *more* rapidly and effectively than their competitors. As pointed out by Pfeffer (1994), this ability and capacity is dependent on the skill and motivation of the workforce. Innovation is crucial here, especially for corporations involved in creating, developing, and applying information technologies.

In my study, many corporations claim that today's markets are demanding that corporations meet myriad tastes and styles simultaneously. It is imperative for companies to employ a cadre of diverse talent that can develop and apply latest technological advances for all markets. As new markets emerge and are permeated, it is the speed with which information technology corporations are responsive to the market that will ultimately determine their competitive advantage.

The successful implementation of business strategies to meet the demands of diverse customers and markets and maintain competitive advantages and innovation encourages the adoption and implementation of diversity strategies. Toward this end, the business imperative of diversity requires organizational activities and practices that seek and obtain employees who mirror the market and are sensitive to and understand customers' wants and needs. Corporations that resist instituting diversity strategies may be unable to respond quickly to new and changing markets and therefore will neglect critical business opportunities, thus risking serious economic harm.

The Pluralistic Imperative

The pluralistic imperative of diversity calls for corporations to institute strategies driven by the mission and values of the company. The primary goal of organizational plurality is simple. It is about the integration of group culture and behavior. Corporations' sensitivity to organizational plurality is motivated by changing workplace demographics. It has been well documented that new entrants to the labor market are becoming more ethnically and racially diverse. In fact, influenced by changing population demographic projections, corporations are moved to institute strategies to not only acquire the skills and talents of women and minorities, but also to implement behaviors to become better prepared for the diverse needs of new and existing employees.

In accord with changing internal demographics, the pluralistic imperative of diversity calls for corporations to establish and push forward bureaucratic control practices that address the professional needs and interests of women and minorities. Specifically, corporations implement activities and programs focused on the development of new skills, career opportunities, and advancement of *individuals*, not groups. These practices are not solely for the sake of improving the individual, but also of increasing corporate performance and productivity.

The pluralistic imperative of diversity dictates that diversity is a systematic function of the corporation. When the word "diversity" is mentioned, it is not foreign. Diversity ideas, goals, and anticipated outcomes are planted throughout the corporation, at all levels. The invisible insignia of diversity is marked by networks and relationships that impact individuals' work experiences. Further, the pluralistic imperative directs corporations to implement strategies that ultimately lead to a critical mass of diverse employees. Shifting attention away from individual groups to individuals taps into the significant richness and specialized talents that diverse populations bring to the company. Practices that nurture leadership and high performance characterize firms concerned with valuing and producing talent that is critical to the corporation.

The enforcement, moral, business, and pluralistic imperatives of diversity represent the external and internal social forces that drive high-performing technology corporations to address and meet their organization goals and objectives. The imperatives, often combined and integrated in many corporations, reflect the primary structures and behaviors of the corporation that, in turn, impact its day-to-day operations. In this view, these imperatives are not unique but specific to the needs and conditions of women and minorities. As vehicles by which strategies and practices are created and applied to the recruitment, hiring, and retention of women and minorities, the enforcement, moral, business, and pluralistic imperatives, then, move corporations toward improvement typically resulting from significant social change outside or within the corporation. The understanding of the enforcement, moral, business, and pluralistic approaches to doing diversity begins with a number of "priorities" that I consider fundamental to effectiveness, flexibility, and change in modern corporations. I believe that these priorities characterize corporations that adopt and implement diversity strategies and, as such, I offer the following terms and descriptions: corporations act, corporations love their customers, corporations as people, value-based corporation, corporations stick to what they do best, and global corporations.

First, *corporations act.* Companies that adopt and implement diversity strategies are not bogged down in bureaucratic practices or hierarchies. They respond to the internal and external environment quickly. Rather than conducting in-depth and lengthy research investigations that generate cumbersome reports, discussions, and meetings, corporations conduct quick and limited experiments to determine the best course of action. Most often, in the case of adopting diversity strategies, corporations assess quickly their relevance to the business objectives. Some determine, without hesitation, their importance not only to immediate goals but also their future place in the global economy.

Corporations' proclivity to action is an antidote to the constraining and dulling efforts of grapping with uncertainty and ambiguity. Waiting for and responding to social forces to serve as full justification for action rarely results in any new structures and behaviors or different visions and directions. Efforts to capitalize on untapped and fresh talent become stagnant and unattainable; new and emerging markets and opportunities are always a goal for the corporation but never a reality. And productivity and innovation remain a difficult challenge for the corporation to master. In essence, corporations that act swiftly, act first. They become the best and top companies for diversity and have little problem recruiting and retaining top women and minority talent in their specific industry. Companies that demonstrate quick action are characteristic of an integration of the enforcement, moral, business, and pluralistic imperatives of diversity.

Corporations love their customers and hold them close. Customers are at the center of every aspect of the corporation. The primary focus here is to meet the needs and demands of current and emerging markets. In this view, corporations that adopt diversity strategies are dependent on the skills and talents of employees that mirror the tastes, preferences, and styles of their customers. Corporations as lovers of the customer flow in a way in which the corporation and people need each other. The production and delivery of products and services is paramount. New and emerging markets and their capability to consume products and services over the long haul motivate the corporation, at every level, to continuously satisfy customers. As such, the corporation keeps its pulse on every segment of the customer base—racial, ethnic, gender, age, disability, sexual orientation, and nationality. Moreover, they are in tune to their socioeconomic and cultural beliefs, behaviors, and conditions, which affects ultimately their desires and preferences for services.

Those corporations that produce services, especially telecommunications/communications, rely on keeping their customers. And, in order to do so, they must be aware of and understand what they want and deliver it in a competitive manner. Intensive sponsorships and philanthropic behaviors are common identifiers of corporations as lovers of the customers. Corporations are actively visible among their customers and are perceived by them as good citizens. They demonstrate appreciation and value toward customers through practices that engender loyalty and sustained patronage. In essence, corporations as lovers of the customer characterize business and moral imperatives.

Corporations as people demonstrate a great need for talent. This need is different from the pursuit of customers. Corporations with diversity strategies need their employees and they tend to implement initiatives to capitalize on untapped talent. They rely heavily on their energy, ideas, and skills. On the other hand, people need the corporation. They need careers, work opportunities, and salaries. However, when the fit between the corporation and its people is poor, both parties suffer. The corporation wastes its resources and performance is inadequate and, conversely, people wind up being exploited and misused.

The need factor in most corporations reveals itself in the autonomous nature and entrepreneurial spirit of employees. Many corporations with diversity strategies are decentralized and broken down into sub-units. They promote practices such as revolving job assignments and offer incentives and rewards that focus on career opportunities rather than salary and income. The work environment is shaped by the innovative process.

It is flexible, low-key, and nonthreatening, and allows for mistakes. It encourages risks. More importantly, the work environment is concerned with individuals rather than groups.

Recognizing individuals' needs and requirements in the workplace contributes to higher productivity and smoother work conditions. Corporations implement structures and practices that identify and meet individuals' needs in order to retain their talents and better prepare the corporation for new entrants. Corporations that are consistently concerned about people use in-house language and resources identifying the importance of individuals, the corporation itself, and its extended affiliates. Employees tend to view the corporation as a "family." Using the family model, the chain of command is informal and the training and socialization of new and current employees is intensive and substantive. Corporation as people characterizes the pluralistic imperative of diversity.

The *value-based corporation* is about its mission and vision. In fact, the corporation's mission and vision is linked strongly to its structures and practices. Products and services are created and based on what the corporation stands for. In most instances, quality, tradition, and experience shape the work environment and its people. Stories, narratives, and myths are a vital part of the corporation. In fact, the lifespan of the corporation is articulated through the telling of stories and narratives.

Corporations' values are transmitted informally but constantly. Major areas or divisions of the corporation have their stories that are inextricably linked to the legacy of the company. Often, stories and narratives are responses to major changes in the corporation that emanate from larger societal forces such as the economy, social movements, and political turmoil. The value-based corporation tends to be among the oldest firms in the country. They demonstrate great pride and longstanding traditions that have lasted for decades. They are prestigious. These corporations insist that their value-based mission and visions are responsible for their longevity and corporate success. They adopt diversity strategies out of a sense of moral obligation and the corporation's sense of history in the United States. Together, the enforcement and moral imperatives are central to the value-based corporation.

Some *corporations stick to what they do best* and avoid becoming conglomerates. Corporations grow by creating new businesses that relate to what they do best. Microsoft stays away from making hamburgers and McDonald's does not produce software. They rarely are involved in the merger and acquisition hysteria that occurs often on Wall Street. They constantly seek to advance and enhance their products while maintaining their reputation for being the best in a certain industry, such as the production of software or research and development.

Firms with diversity strategies are *corporations that stick to what they do best* and are very specific about their labor needs. They seek serious individuals with specialized skills and knowledge, and find these attributes are especially true in the case of women and minority talent. Firms are highly competitive and innovative. Their growth hinges on developing new products and services regularly. Structures of the corporation tend to be loose and fluid. In most instances, all areas of the company work collaboratively and are dependent on each other for production and services. Many of these corporations recognize that a jack of all trades is a master of none. They are conscious of new opportunities and are convinced that they would undoubtedly distract them from advancing their current production and services. Indeed, these corporations illustrate how business strategy is imperative to their approaches.

Loose and *tight coupling* refers to corporations with diversity strategies that combine high levels of centralized and decentralized control. Simply put, corporations can have it both ways. Coupling refers to the notion that anything can be tied together in the corporation and has a broad range. For example, performance indicators may be tied to decisions or goals, actors coupled with actors, sub-units coupled with sub-units, and systems coupled with systems. Loose coupling means that corporations have autonomous groups. They are sensitive to environmental changes and tend to adapt to conflict at the institutional level. Adaptation generally means that there are conflicting demands by the environment.

For some corporations with diversity strategies, loose coupling is evident when structural changes occur and there is yet a commitment on the part of the corporation to external constituents, regardless of the effectiveness of the new structure. Employees communicate through several levels of hierarchy rather than directly with one another.

In contrast, many corporations with diversity strategies demonstrate tight coupling. Tight coupling means that structural arrangements represent mechanisms and behavior within a corporation. These mechanisms are formal and task-related and are modified only through formal decisions. They reflect formal hierarchy, rules, and differentiation and integration. Prescribed, conscious, and planned activities demonstrate tightly coupled corporations.

Corporations with diversity strategies that employ both loose and tight coupling are closely guided by their mission and vision. They tend to rely on formal and informal structures. However, their formal structures do not solely mean tight coupling. Some mechanisms such as decentralization, delegation, and professionalization are methods to bring looseness and flexibility into the corporation. These mechanisms are desirable and serve as a positive means of responding to conflicting demands from the environment. Loose and tight coupling thus characterize corporations' imperatives to do business, to be moral and pluralistic, and to enforce legal mandates.

Lastly, many corporations with diversity strategies are characterized as *global corporations*, or transnational corporations. They manage production establishments and investments or deliver services in two or more countries. Many global corporations have great influence in international relations and local economies. Also, they play an extraordinary role in globalization. Without a doubt, global corporations locate in countries outside the United States to gain access to foreign markets, pay low costs for production facilities, and acquire an abundance of skilled and inexpensive labor. Global corporations are diversified in that they manage a wide range of proprietary and specialized products to multiple markets.

The management of global corporations differs from that of domestic ones and they, too, have their own issues. In particular, fundamental foreign, economic, strategic, organizational, and sociopolitical issues have a significant impact on the foreign expansion of the firm, and on the linkages between foreign subsidiaries and corporate headquarters in the home country. The relationship between global corporations and interest groups in foreign countries, including the government, labor unions, and suppliers, are just a few areas of grave concern.

Global corporations exist because economic conditions make it possible for their products or services to be profitable in a foreign land. There are three major economic aspects of global corporations. First, foreign investment tends to occur more frequently among corporations that compete in an oligopoly in the home country. Second, the process of foreign expansion is often, though not always, driven by product life-cycle dynamics. In other words, corporations seem to come up with new product ideas and services based on stimuli from the home country. And third, global corporations benefit from their "multinationality" in that it is only companies in several countries that can use their network of subsidiaries to arbitrate differences in prices or adverse stocks such as sudden currency realignment.

Assuming there is competitive advantage over domestic companies, there are two fundamental strategic decisions made by global corporations. First, the corporation decides where to locate its assets and employees. This decision is almost purely economic and results in whether or not a corporation is more or less geographically dispersed throughout the world. Second, if the corporation is dispersed throughout the world, it determines if there is a need for managerial coordination. Depending on the degree of geographical dispersion and organizational coordination, global corporations are likely to be less decentralized. It is important to understand that the degree of dispersion and coordination is continuous in nature and not dichotomous.

Corporations located in two or more countries typically use the "teamwork" or "network" approach. They are less bureaucratic in hierarchy and more flexible. Communication, for example, is independent of hierarchy in global corporations. In fact, information technologies are significant in global corporations. A wealth of communication takes place by computer. Some scholars claim that global corporations have forged the end of bureaucracy and the rise of the intelligent corporation.

Key issues facing global corporations include local responsiveness, global integration, the dynamics of local interest groups in foreign countries, and the corporations' relative bargaining power. In particular, global corporations must implement strategies across the border. This requires companies to exploit new opportunities that will ensure competitive advantage over domestic companies. In this case, the mastery of international situations results in corporations' successful expansion throughout the world. Because of the emphasis on economic strategy and coordination throughout the world, global corporations are highly characterized by the business imperative.

The seven priorities of high-performing information technology corporations characterize the principles and central tenets that underpin the enforcement, moral, business, and pluralistic imperatives of diversity. Corporations' traditions, values, philosophies, strategies, and histories are reflected in these priorities. In turn, these priorities lay the groundwork for corporations to establish enforcement, moral, business, and pluralistic approaches to adopt diversity strategies.

A crisp and clear understanding of how one factor motivates corporations to adopt diversity strategies has little relevance in a messy world of uncertainty, unpredictability, and instability. Economic times that resemble a recession are likely to encourage any formal actions toward implementing strategies concerning women and minorities. Many researchers and business leaders note how the business imperative is the driving force for adopting and implementing diversity strategies. However, it is important to understand that, when combined, the enforcement, moral, business, and pluralistic imperatives are very effective in negotiating the hiring and retaining of women and minorities.

Often, I am asked which imperative is the most important in a corporation's decision to adopt and implement diversity strategies. It was not until the writing of this book that I became clear that the answer is not about which imperative, but rather about which organizational variable is most important to help determine the imperative more likely to be effective in any given situation. Some key organizational variables associated with the motivation of corporations' decisions to adopt diversity strategies are motivation, leadership, technical constraints, uncertainty, scarcity, and conflict.

Recognizing that social forces also remain important to corporations when considering strategies to recruit and retain women and minorities, effective and high-performing companies rely on them to push forward imperatives that reflect their structures and behaviors as well as their mission and values. Although each of the four imperatives generates a different strategy or practice for attracting women and minority talent, depending on their social, economic, and political environments at a particular point in time, corporations can enhance their flexibility and freedom. Each imperative provides a guideline for leading corporations to action and even to different results, although applied to the same goal. Therefore, I believe that the appropriate pathway to workforce inclusion is to hold each imperative of diversity equal in its perception of importance in order to meet and go beyond corporations' and society's expectations and experiences.

Chapter Nine

Small battles [against discrimination] are being won around the world, but, I think people are losing. I do see the present and the future of our children as very dark. But I trust the people's capacity for reflection, rage, and rebellion.

—Oscar Olivera, leader of the protest against water privatization in Bolivia

Chapter Nine
The Business of Diversity

During the time of this study, there is no doubt that corporate America has improved its efforts at creating a more inclusive environment at the CEO and boardroom levels. Given the recent selections of Lloyd Ward, the first African American CEO of a Fortune 500 company, the Maytag Corporation; Franklin Raines, CEO of the Fannie Mae Corporation, the second African American to head up a Fortune 500 company; Kenneth Chenault, the first African American to helm a Dow Jones blue chip company, American Express; Richard Parsons, the first African American to guide Time Warner, a major media conglomerate; Brandy Thomas, CEO of Cyveillance, an online business brand monitoring service; and Stanley O'Neal, at the helm of Merrill Lynch; many agree that minorities, African Americans, in particular, are, at least, represented. Comparatively, female CEOs have not fared nearly as well. However, the appointments of Carly Fiorina, the only female and former CEO of a Fortune 500 company, the Hewlett-Packard Corporation, a Top 30 technology firm located on the Dow Jones; and Nancy Stetson, the first female CEO of Public Broadcasting Services (PBS); may have shattered the glass ceiling for women in corporate America. In fact, management seems to have its own flavor and behavior concerning women and minorities. There are visible efforts to ensure that these groups have opportunities to assume leadership positions and be counted among the nation's corporate elites. But the story does not end here.

Although many corporations feel strongly that they are becoming more inclusive environments, many female and minority professionals are not convinced. Today, an overwhelming number of Fortune 500 companies employ diversity programs. However, critics claim that the large majority of these programs are "the flavor of the day," "superficial," "cosmetic," "a form of window dressing," "quick hits," or make "symbolic and unreal" efforts at achieving diversity. Over the past year, myriad publications ranging from newspaper and magazine articles to scholarly journal articles and books have criticized corporate diversity initiatives as having an illusion of inclusion. They are not as effective as companies claim. Influenced by such observations, my work sought to explore and explain why and how corporations adopt diversity strategies focused on women and minority information technology professionals. In order to accomplish this, it was necessary to investigate the corporation itself—to assess its diversity structures and behaviors, those associated with both the external environment and internal organizational arrangements. It was important to begin with the critical issue at hand—hiring difficulties and conditions as experienced by the corporation.

In general, as suggested by a wealth of data provided in national reports, corporations are indeed experiencing *more* difficulty recruiting and hiring women and minorities compared to their white and male counterparts. However, a closer investigation of firms' characteristics shed light on the degree to which corporations differ in their recruitment and hiring difficulties of women and minority talent.

It is important to understand that a certain group of corporations are more likely to experience similar difficulties in recruiting and hiring women and minorities. Younger corporations that do not adopt diversity strategies, located in the South and classified as systems analyses and engineering companies, tend to experience more problems recruiting and hiring women and minorities. These corporations also strongly favor certain conditions for employing these groups. They require formal education in a technology-related discipline leading to at least a bachelor's degree and, for the most part, they tend to employ a majority of women and minorities with formal education and professional training in highly specialized, technical fields.

In contrast, corporations with diversity strategies are *less* likely to experience difficulty in employing women and minorities. That is, the presence of diversity strategies is associated with more successful recruitment and hiring of women and minorities. Differing from corporations without diversity initiatives, these companies are older, wealthier, located in the Northeast or Midwest, and classified as software development and programming industries. These corporate profiles are neither random nor are they meaningless.

Older corporations have historically implemented strategies to increase the proportions of women and minorities due to racial riots, boycotts, and lawsuits during the 1960s and early 1970s. The passage of Affirmative Action programs and Equal Employment Opportunity legislation is also a great motivator of corporations' adoption of diversity strategies. Thus, older corporations have an established reputation for consistently employing women and minorities over the past four decades. It is not surprising that these corporations are located in the Northeast and Midwest regions of the country. During the period of American industrialization, several older technology-related corporations were established in the Northeast. Later, corporations sprang up in or relocated to the Midwest due to economic expansion. However, it was only during the past decade or so, with the information technology boom, that technology-related corporations began to emerge in the southern and western regions of the U.S. In fact, corporations classified primarily as software developers and programmers are among the earliest to emerge in the technology sector. Software development and programming have encompassed decades of programming languages, technologies, operating systems, and user interfaces. Simply put, older technology corporations have had the lion's share of dealing with the issue of workplace diversity. The enforcement and moral imperatives have shaped their structures and behaviors to adopt and implement diversity strategies over the years. As such, their trouble with attracting and hiring women and minorities is not as great as that of younger corporations who claim that all is well in a color-blind society.

What is discovered here is relevant. Although there exists a wealth of reports indicating that corporations are struggling to find qualified women and minority talent, very little information is provided on how information technology corporations might differ in their recruitment and hiring experiences of women and minorities. Moreover, very little information exists on the types of corporations that experience the greatest recruiting and hiring challenges. These results provide a better understanding of corporations that fail to adopt diversity strategies. They also provide a glimpse of those features that characterize corporations that experience less difficulty employing women and minorities.

It is necessary to consider the history of a corporation's efforts to pursue diversity. Responding to a series of crises ranging from racial riots to class-action discrimination suits prepares corporations to pursue diversity. The absence or lack of experience in responding to such crises contributes to corporations' challenges and difficulties in employing women and minorities. Perhaps there are no other forces that have shaped the behaviors of corporations in employing women and minorities than the federal courts and the freedom to protest. Without the experiences of such social forces to guide corporations' employment policies and practices, companies may find themselves scrambling to create beneficial approaches to ensuring workplace diversity. However, the majority of corporations in the United States that have been publicly recognized for their outstanding efforts in the area of workplace diversity were guided by one approach—Affirmative Action programs.

It is necessary to determine the motivations of corporations' diversity structures and behaviors by assessing the extent to which the state influences the adoption of diversity strategies. In line with institutionalist thinking, Affirmative Action and Equal Opportunity policies are associated with the adoption and implementation of corporations' diversity initiatives. The *timing* with which diversity behaviors made their hallmark across the country is important. In the presence of the political backlash against Affirmative Action programs was the emergence of most corporations' formal diversity strategies. Clearly, there is an important link between Affirmative Action programs and diversity structures and behaviors. Diversity behaviors support and encourage Affirmative Action sentiments. Rather than prohibiting workplace discrimination based on age, color, disability, veteran status, national origin, race, religion, and gender, the dimensions of diversity offer no specific guidelines for correcting historic patterns of discrimination once they are identified within the workplace. As opposed to *requiring* corporations not to discriminate, diversity softens the blow; it *encourages* the inclusion of *all* individuals and not just groups.

Operationally, however, diversity strategies seem to vary among corporations. Diversity activities range from an emphasis on traditional Affirmative Action and Equal Employment Opportunity programs to an extension to the community and the world. Diversity activities are justified by a range of explanations such as "It's the right thing to do," "It's the law," "The CEO wants it," and "It makes good business sense." In essence, corporations are reliant upon basic standard justifications which shaped, directed, and guided their diversity practices. Going after women and minorities is not done in a vacuum; it requires a justifiable reason, an explanation.

Affirmative Action, *not* diversity, is used to *create* a diverse workplace and to provide upward mobility for women and minorities. In turn, *diversity* structures and behaviors call for mutual respect among diverse groups and increased receptivity of Affirmative Action. In this view, many corporations assert that diversity goes *beyond* EEO/AA. It goes beyond the tenets of AA. It is the next step in the organization's evolution to becoming totally inclusive. Under the human resources model, diversity strategies are very broad. They benefit the corporation. Their immediate goals are to seek, attract, develop, advance, and retain the best talent. Corporations use diversity strategies in their drive to become an employer of choice among a diverse population, and as a means to create an environment that benefits individuals, not groups, throughout the corporation. However, diversity efforts within the corporation are generally misunderstood by those outside the organization. This is evidenced by popular criticisms of diversity initiatives over the past several years. When the principles, sentiments, and ideals of Affirmative Action *and* diversity are combined, backlash, resistance, and even polarization ensue.

Arguably, Affirmative Action and Equal Employment Opportunity build upon each other. However, once Affirmative Action and diversity are *tied* together, diversity becomes tainted in two significant ways. First, it becomes smeared by negative perceptions of Affirmative Action and its accusations of reverse discrimination, and secondly, diversity is usually criticized and dismissed by Affirmative Action proponents as "window dressing." Hence, this relationship is somewhat problematic. It seems to draw on each other's weaknesses rather than strengths. No wonder academicians and practitioners are questioning the effectiveness of corporate diversity practices to increase the number of women and minorities. Nevertheless, conclusions can be made about diversity strategies that are alive and well. Undoubtedly, corporations have shifted the power of Affirmative Action to affirming diversity.

Most corporations assert that diversity strategies are characterized in two ways. First, diversity prescribes a change in the individual's *thinking*; it proposes a shift in mindset as well as systematic change. Philosophically, diversity is a *valued* aspect of the corporation. Its main objective includes awareness, education, and positive recognition for individual differences. As a valued aspect of a corporation's culture, diversity structures and behaviors seek to recognize the uniqueness of all employees, thereby creating an inclusive environment where individuals are respected and promoted *because* of their differences. It is important to note here that it is simply the *quality* of the work experience that is paramount, rather than the participation rates of women and minority employees. This is an incredibly different agenda from that posed by Affirmative Action practices. In essence, this pluralistic imperative of diversity encourages prime behaviors such as innovation and entrepreneurship.

Second, corporations believe that diversity is about business—capitalizing on that which contributes to the corporations' goals and objectives associated with profits and productivity. It is an approach to doing business that is aligned with other organizational goals. In this view, my research demonstrates a repeated theme for most corporations— "diversity makes good business sense." Against the backdrop of changing demographics, this principle means that most corporations implement diversity structures and behaviors in two important ways: internally and externally. First, within the corporation, diversity behaviors are sought to influence the creation of an inclusive work environment by attracting and retaining a diverse group of talented people. Of equal importance is the fact that the corporations' diversity practices are used to reduce risk and uncertainty associated with grievances, complaints, and lawsuits that demonstrate vulnerability to legal sanctions.

Outside the corporation, diversity efforts are primarily focused on a growing and changing marketplace. Demographic changes in a corporation's customer base are interpreted as new opportunities for different products, services and, of course, increased profits. And, finally, a corporation's image is considered very important. Limiting and avoiding negative perceptions and experiences in the marketplace concerning "diversity" is crucial given the high cost of lost customers and markets. In turn, it is vital to be perceived as a "good corporate citizen" who values diversity. Corporate social responsibility remains an important aspect of organizational performance. As participants in the global marketplace, corporations can no longer afford to negate or be passive in their responses to social issues in a society that requires, at least to some degree, their involvement.

Diversity policies are important in formally framing the foundation of diversity structures and behaviors. They generally include not only a statement of how the corporation defines diversity, but these statements also stress nondiscrimination, equality, and fairness. It is at this juncture that the matter of diversity is usually associated or confused with Affirmative Action and Equal Employment Opportunity. They share a familiar sentiment and desired outcome. However, diversity, in scope and purpose, is *not* a form of, substitute for, or variation of Affirmative Action. Nonetheless, this proposition begets a serious question: Can corporations do diversity *without* the support of Affirmative Action or, more broadly, enacting structures and behaviors to ensure the proportional representation of women and minorities in the labor market? I conclude, from findings in this study, that the answer is "probably not."

Because corporations in general in the U.S. are continuing to struggle with the hiring, promotion, and retention of underrepresented groups and often fall short of their goals to do so, Affirmative Action remains crucial in aiding corporations to recognize and develop untapped and underrepresented talent. Put simply, most corporations and work organizations are not there yet. Without mandates to *ensure* the development of a plan focused on women and minorities, many organizations would probably experience great difficulty in attracting and retaining talented women and minorities. It would not surprise me if a significant number of work organizations, in sheer frustration, would simply "give up the race." However, I do firmly believe that there are men and women committed to ensuring that America's corporations represent severely underrepresented groups such as women and minorities. In this view, diversity strategies have great potential and utility in the workplace. They can only help.

Serving as an important complement to Affirmative Action practices, diversity strategies have the potential for *preparing* corporations to receive individuals whom they value into the workplace. In this context, diversity functions quite differently from Affirmative Action. For it is entirely possible that a corporation may obtain proportionality of women and minorities but fail to demonstrate that group and individual differences are *valued*. And, the lack of valuation ultimately leads to retention issues. While diversity is conceptualized as a component of value of most corporations, it is also positioned as a means of serving innovation, marketing, and product needs. Put simply, diversity is leveraged for increasing corporations' productivity and competitive advantage.

The perceived link between Affirmative Action and diversity is important to understand given that many corporations provide each area with autonomy and resources to pursue their own separate, although at times integrated, goals and objectives. Internally as well as externally, corporations attempt to communicate that diversity is a *complement* to Affirmative Action and Equal Employment Opportunity; it is not a replacement or substitute for them. Because diversity strategies appear to be flexible, creative, and changing, corporations create and test activities focused on removing barriers of discrimination, thus encouraging equality and proportionality not prescribed by legal mandates of nondiscrimination in the purview of Affirmative Action and Equal Employment Opportunity.

Corporations claim that diversity strategies, *not* Affirmative Action, are important aspects of their business initiatives and organizational culture. Therefore, it is crucial to avoid misconceptions or misunderstandings of the relationship between Affirmative Action and diversity. Often, corporations make a demonstrated effort to make clear the distinction between Affirmative Action and other traditional approaches to workplace inclusion and diversity.

The way in which corporations can successfully maintain the separate identities of Affirmative Action programs and diversity strategies is to create separate organizational functions. Although sharing common goals, each program is physically located in separate offices with distinct programmatic efforts and purposes as well as methods of implementation. Separate managers or directors are an excellent means of establishing distinct reporting lines. These efforts are likely to prevent possible tension, conflict, and confusion associated with each program's similar goals and objectives.

Last, as required by law for Affirmative Action programs, diversity strategies are evaluated in an effort to determine outcomes. Are corporations meeting their diversity goals and objectives? Which diversity strategy is successful and which unsuccessful? Which strategy is most fundamental and basic to the corporation? And, when is it necessary to revitalize, reevaluate, and redesign a corporation's diversity structures and behaviors? Systematically, evaluative methods tend to be incorporated throughout the entire organization, not only in the area in which the programs and activities originate. In addition to numerical analyses, employees' perceptions and experiences are assessed to gather more detailed information on the challenges, limitations, and improvements of corporations' diversity efforts.

Perceptions of legal mandates and their impact on the adoption and implementation of diversity strategies provide a fuller understanding of the structures and behaviors that shape decisions and practices geared toward attracting and retaining women and minority talent. Recognizing the complications that are inherent in the relationship between federal employment policies and corporate practices provides an important lens for assessing why corporations develop strategies to bring in and keep women and minorities. Understanding the experiences of corporations then leads to understanding their actions. Corporate actions on women and minority issues are critically important for understanding the practices employed and resources used to actively recruit and hire highly qualified and trained women and minority talent.

There are two primary sources of women and minority science and engineering talent—colleges and universities and science and engineering professional associations. In particular, established and maintained formal relationships with women and minority colleges and universities and women and minority science and engineering professional associations are important in the successful recruitment and hiring of women and minority talent. However, corporations claim that developing and maintaining relationships with both sources is *not* an effective means of recruiting and hiring women and minorities.

Resource dependence thinking assumes that corporations that are dependent upon the environment for an increased number of women and minorities will adopt diversity strategies. In other words, the presence of diversity strategies translates into organizational ties and partnerships with women and minority institutions and organizations. But most relevant to corporations with diversity initiatives are women and minority colleges and universities and women and minority science and engineering groups.

My work captures the *changing* and complicated relationships among certain historically black colleges and universities (HBCUs), women and minority science and engineering groups, and, of course, the mighty corporation. In essence, corporate relationships with HBCUs and women and minority science and engineering groups are primarily financial. From the perspective of the corporation, ties with certain HBCUs and women and minority science and engineering groups rarely result in the successful recruitment of women and minority IT talent. This was not the case two or three decades ago. Significantly influenced by legal mandates and government policies to ensure fair representation of women and minorities, the vast majority of corporations flocked to HBCUs hoping to employ many of the nation's best and brightest minority students. Today, corporations' attention has shifted to other viable sources of women and minority talent.

HBCUs' attitudes and behaviors toward corporations are quite common. Generally speaking, because certain HBCUs are frequently faced with serious financial burdens, corporations are seen as a legitimate means of reducing an institution's financial hardships through financial contributions and sponsorship. HBCUs' preoccupation with securing financial resources from corporations has resulted in minimal efforts to establish long-term and substantive relationships focused on students' career opportunities and faculty research. Consequently, ties with certain HBCUs have become one-sided—benefiting financially the HBCU. Conversely, corporations report with much frustration that there is "no return on their investments." The same is found to be true in the case of women and minority science and engineering groups. Corporations point out that the nature of the relationship with women and minority science and engineering professional groups is, again, financial. For many of these groups, corporate sponsorships are life-savers. They allow these organizations to conduct their major activities, such as hosting conferences and workshops and disseminating relevant materials to its membership.

Over the past few years, corporations with diversity strategies tend to shy away from certain HBCUs. They are also reluctant to enter into relationships with women and minority science and engineering groups. Recently, with the nation's economic downturn, it has become increasingly difficult for many corporations to justify continued sponsorship of and participation in programs and activities held at certain HBCU institutions or by certain women and minority science and engineering organizations. Put simply, under the business principle of diversity, no longer are corporations capable of allocating resources to certain HBCUs and women and minority science and engineering groups *without* getting some return on their investments. One corporation indicated that it used to recruit at twenty-two HBCUs; that list has been reduced to eight. The decision to do so was a strategic one.

As discussed in Chapter 3, corporations' perceptions of women's and minorities' preparation for the workforce is critical. The majority of corporations having the greatest problems hiring women and minorities perceive these groups as being lesser qualified for entry into the corporation. This conclusion is crucial for HBCUs given that they graduate a significant proportion of minority students with degrees in technical fields. In many instances, corporations question the rigor of certain HBCUs' technology-related academic programs. They have questions about academic standards, achievement, and the necessary exposure and training minority students ought to have prior to graduation. Are HBCU students adequately educated to pursue technology careers in corporate America? Are they truly the best and the brightest among other job candidates in their racial and ethnic groups? Many corporations are attempting to answer these questions.

Realizing the narrow focus and limitations of recruiting primarily for minority students at HBCUs, corporations have begun to seek additional ways to identify and recruit them. Corporations are beginning to establish substantive relationships with predominantly white colleges and universities with diverse student bodies majoring in technology-related disciplines. These institutions are becoming favored options for many companies given that their technology programs are nationally ranked and their women and minority students participate in highly competitive internships and training programs. In most cases, corporations' relationships with predominantly white colleges and universities are not premised on financial support or sponsorships.

Because corporations are recruiting more and more at white colleges and universities, this raises the issue that it is likely that minority students enrolled in HBCUs may ultimately be *excluded* from career opportunities in some of America's leading technology firms. Therefore, it is incumbent upon HBCUs to enter into successful and positive relationships with corporations to ensure that their students are provided the same career and employment opportunities as non-minority students enrolled in predominantly white colleges and universities.

It is important to realize as well that corporations are turning inward to attract and hire women and minority talent. In other words, they understand that key information for attracting a broader array of employees may be found among existing employees. A host of corporations enlist support in recruiting qualified and talented women and minorities by offering employee referral bonuses. No longer are recruitment efforts limited to or focused outside the organization. In fact, it is becoming commonplace for corporations with diversity strategies to use employee referrals in the recruiting and hiring of women and minorities. This strategy is proving to be beneficial to the corporation in that employees tend to recruit individuals with similar values, work ethics, and motivation, all positive attributes for competitive and high-performing technology companies.

Alternative and strong sources of women and minority talent may be problematic for HBCUs, in particular. Interorganizational ties are especially crucial for HBCUs. Throughout the nation's higher education system, 16 percent of 1.4 million African Americans are enrolled in one of the nation's one hundred five HBCUs (National Center of Education Statistics 2008). Clearly, these colleges and universities compose a hefty proportion of African American students. Hence, it is vital for HBCUs to continually re-examine themselves in relation to their current and future relationships with corporate partners and sponsors. This effort might call for a reassessment of their institution's mission and role in society in general.

Traditionally, the role and impact of HBCUs have been felt deeply in the African American community and in the nation as a whole. HBCUs have produced and continue to produce leaders in the African American community, they stimulate the interests of African American youth in higher education, they serve as custodians for the archives of African Americans, they develop learning methodologies for overcoming handicaps of the educationally disadvantaged, they develop and expand programs for educating African American adults, and they provide educational opportunities for students who fall short of admissions requirements of conventional institutions of higher learning (Carnegie Commission on Higher Education Report 1971). Although this unique history remains important today, perhaps for some HBCUs it may serve as an obstacle to or pose difficulties in establishing and maintaining substantive relationships with corporations. The historical foundation of HBCUs might be in conflict with the spirit and essence of the mighty corporation. HBCUs and corporate structures and behaviors simply do not mirror each other. So, perhaps cultivating such relationships is not in the general purview of certain HBCUs for several reasons. They struggle with limited personnel, inexperience, lack of faculty involvement, and limited academic and student resources. These factors are imperative to corporations as they, too, struggle, but do so in order to remain globally competitive and generate profits.

A careful review of over fifty women and minority science and engineering professional groups' membership brochures and related materials indicates that the purpose and function of such organizations are multiple. For example, they are purposed to stimulate women and minority interest in science, technology, and engineering; to increase the number of women and minority scientists and engineers; to promote public awareness of women and minorities' involvement in science, technology, and engineering; to offer tutorial services and technical seminars and workshops; to provide a national communications network, national magazines, newsletters, and other correspondence; to sponsor national meetings and conferences; to provide online-based job advertisements and announcements; to offer scholarships and financial assistance to women and minorities in science, technology, and engineering; and to provide women and minorities coaching and professional training opportunities in information technology.

Certainly, the work of most women and minority science and engineering professional groups is critical to the emergence, development, and professional advancement of women and minority students and professionals. In fact, several groups, such as the National Society of Black Engineers, Catalysts, Women in Technology, and the National Society of Hispanic Professional Engineers, have been recognized nationally for their outstanding contributions in the fields of science and engineering. It is evident that such organizations have the potential to be exceptionally helpful in improving the entry, training, and retention of women and minorities in information technology.

Substantive and positive relationships between women and minority science and engineering professional organizations should involve an articulation of what the industry wants and needs. By listening to and understanding the needs of employers, women and minority science and engineering organizations can be useful to industry. For example, many associations can translate the needs of industry by focusing on and evaluating technology-related curricula in women and minority colleges and universities. Such efforts might improve the attractiveness of certain women and minority colleges and universities as well as the employment qualifications of prospective job candidates. Also, women and minority science and engineering groups can play a crucial role in enhancing the professional training of women and minority professionals. This may serve not only their members but corporations as well in their efforts to train and retain women and minorities. Because the nature of information technology work usually requires ongoing and continuous training, women and minority science and engineering professional groups should take an active role in developing and implementing their continuing education programs to ensure that their members have opportunities for continuous and relevant IT training. These activities may encourage corporations not only to continue their financial support and sponsorship of these groups but also to be important sources of career and work opportunities for the long haul of an individual's work life. This will allow corporations to move beyond the simple action of demonstrating moral and corporate social responsibility to actively engaging in increasing the presence of women and minorities in the firm.

Today, the external environment is critical to the lifespan of the corporation. In fact, it is continuously dependent on it for its critical resources. Diversity strategies designed to bring in women and minorities are driven by the environment. Legal mandates, whether in the form of Affirmative Action programs or corporate diversity initiatives, remain a huge factor in corporations' decisions to adopt and implement practices to seek out and retain women and minority talent. Interorganizational ties are instrumental in how corporations attempt to bring them in. Although there is an important shift in the means of obtaining women and minorities, corporations continue to demonstrate new ways to improve their efforts at identifying and hiring the best talent.

If institutionalist and interorganizationalist approaches are useful concepts in understanding corporations' diversity strategies, then bureaucratic control theory is absolutely critical for exploring the impact of internal organizational factors on the presence of diversity structures. Similar to the findings on the role of the state and interorganizational relationships, here again, the contribution to theory provides background for practice.

As discussed so far, recruitment and hiring practices associated with diversity strategies are influenced by and implemented outside the corporation. However, there is overlap. There are some hiring activities that tend to emanate from inside the corporation. As for retention practices, practically all these activities originate and are implemented within the company. It is important to recognize that there is no cookie-cutter style of implementing diversity strategies. Given its nature and multiple dimensions, diversity strategies should be flexible, creative, and changing as they are inextricably linked to and shaped by the external and organizational environments.

Hiring and retention practices directed toward women and minorities are not usually confined by corporations' diversity structures. What I mean by this is that they are not owned by a particular department, for example, the likely entity, human resources management. Instead, most hiring and retention activities are a function of specific business units, for instance, benefits, compensation, recruitment, and work/life. In contrast, most corporations describe their human resources management functions very broadly. They are responsible for planning and allocating resources, developing an environment in which employees choose motivation and contribution, leading organizational efforts to listen to and serve customers, and setting examples in work ethics, empowerment, and treatment of people worthy of being emulated by others.

Because hiring and retention activities are then owned by multiple business units, diversity *values*—its principles, sentiments and goals—are incorporated throughout the corporation by placing individuals with diversity responsibilities within each primary business area. The primary responsibility of these individuals is to act as advocates, ensuring that their respective units are in accordance with the corporation's overall diversity guidelines and goals. In most instances, when this is the case, each business unit is given a target diversity goal in line with the corporations' business objectives. For example, the research and development unit may be required to increase the number of women junior analysts by 5 percent within a two-year period.

Surprisingly, traditional hiring and retention-type practices are not the activities of choice for corporations. The implementation of professional training programs, support groups, on-the-job training, rotating job assignments, financial incentives and bonuses, or continuing education programs is not primary in hiring and retaining women and minority employees. Rather, it appears that a corporation's reputation and established record of promoting and advancing women and minorities are the best tools for increasing the number of women and minorities.

In terms of retaining employees specifically, in the spirit of bureaucratic control theory, financial incentives and job promotions are important. These rewards are likely to encourage employee loyalty and avoid early departure from the corporation. However, women and minority scientists and engineers remain with the corporation when they experience positive relationships with management. Supportive and favorable relationships with their supervisors tend to hide a multitude of sins. It is not unusual for women and minorities to excuse other organizational flaws if they are satisfied with their immediate relationships such as those with their bosses. Equally important, women and minorities choose to stay with a corporation when they experience and participate in challenging and innovative work assignments. Rotating, especially, in the information technology world creates new and improved opportunities for growth and learning rather than merely a change in status or span of authority.

Although the nation's economic downturn and seesawing demand for information technology employees have impacted greatly the information technology sector, there is still a need for corporations to continuously pursue a well-trained and qualified workforce. Over the past several years, labor researchers and relevant national research organizations have produced a wealth of reports and scholarly work aimed at recruiting and retaining technology intense employees. These important works address salary, training, career promotion and progression, job descriptions and titles, formalized business policies, strategic plans, foreign labor, women and minorities, and data measurements. Although common in many ways, this wide range of issues has its own particularities to the information technology sector. As such, there is much fertile ground for exploring corporations' behaviors in capitalizing on the unique role of women and minority scientists and engineers.

Because the responsibility for implementing strategies to hire and retain women and minorities does not reside with only one office, it is essential that corporations monitor and evaluate diversity behaviors throughout the entire organization. Accountability is crucial here. Employers and employees should understand clearly that "everyone is responsible," but managers are accountable. Diversity performance should include performance objectives and measures, and appropriate skills should be acquired in order to establish and maintain relationships with diverse customers. Diverse management teams should be created and senior managers should recruit and mentor diverse groups of employees. It is crucial that an individual manager's performance objectives are linked to the corporation's diversity goals. And, as discussed earlier, offering financial incentives as a reward when meeting one's diversity-related performance objectives is an excellent means of ensuring that managers "do diversity."

Although traditional hiring and retention-type activities such as increased salaries and benefits may be the chosen method of retaining employees, in this work, it does not take center stage as the reason or remedy for attracting and retaining highly qualified women and minorities. Creating a work environment where women and minorities are demonstrably valued and challenged and experience positive relationships with management is more beneficial over time.

The retention of women and minority employees is not only good for the individual but also for the employer. Retained women and minority employees contribute to a corporation's reputation and image of *valuing* diversity and acting affirmatively to ensure equity in employment opportunities. Certainly, work relationships are important and occur among all members of the corporation. Employees, by default, are bound together in an organization. They are a common denominator regardless of race, gender, age, or other dimensions of diversity. However, the quality and quantity of relationships vary and are much affected by an individual's diverse background.

As suggested by one human resources professional, there are a number of creative ways to increase the retention of women and minority employees. Simple but creative efforts that recognize the issues of geography and quality of living are important. For example, providing one or two airplane tickets per year to return "home"; pre-paid long-distance calling cards; and gift cards to barber shops or hair salons and restaurants specializing in ethnic foods are all good corporate behaviors that can contribute to the positive valuation of women and minority employees. As most employees would agree, "If you love me, show me!"

It is not uncommon to smile or feel good when minorities see each other in a predominantly white work environment—especially in the mighty, white male-dominated corporation. The presence of someone who looks like you tends to ease some anxiousness about being the "only one." After all, this is what results from being a top diversity employer. Individuals feel good about who they see in the corporation. They are inclined to want to work there and remain there. Similar faces based on racial and ethnic backgrounds are a welcome mat to potential employees. As they say, "If you build it, they will come."

A small number of research studies have devoted attention to neoinstitutionalists' arguments of *professionals as agents of diffusion*. This model provides an important approach for examining the relationship between the presence of women and minority human resources professionals and women and minority scientists and engineers and the adoption of diversity strategies. Indeed, the presence of women and minority human resources managers is related to the existence of diversity strategies. Corporations benefit from these HR managers in that they are committed to the company's diversity goals and tend to go above and beyond to ensure that their female and minority counterparts are present and treated fairly in the corporation. Supporting the work of Kanter (1977), there is an association between the proportion of women and minority employees and the presence of diversity structures. Corporations that adopt and implement diversity strategies have higher proportions of women and minority scientists and engineers.

The link between the presence of diversity strategies and a greater proportion of women and minority employees is important for corporations who strive to increase their numbers of these groups. This concludes that diversity initiatives employed by the corporation contribute to or result in a greater proportion of women and minorities. Although formalized, personnel functions and responsibilities helmed by women and minority human resources managers are an ideal means of successfully hiring and retaining women and minorities, it is important to note that perhaps it only requires a critical mass of these groups to attract and retain diverse populations.

Although the major thrust of my work was to explore why and how corporations adopt diversity strategies, much more has been revealed. My research illuminates corporations' difficulties and experiences in hiring women and minorities; the changing nature and complicated relationship between corporations and women and minority organizations; the relevance of less formalized, nontraditional bureaucratic labor practices; and the significant impact of the presence of women and minorities on the adoption of corporations' diversity structures and behaviors.

Throughout American history, diversity, be it racial, ethnic, or gender based, has been a part of the human condition. Today, diversity, as a concept, has reached beyond what would have been imagined years ago. The workplace serves to reflect the dynamic, dramatic, global, and, at times, devastating effects of and responses to diverse populations. As such, diversity offers the opportunity for tremendous change in organizational structures and personal ideologies. Besides advancing technologies, the single most important factor impacting the workplace is the nation's changing demographics.

As discussed throughout this book, diversity spans the corporation in many ways—human resources, customers and clients, employers, employees, community, and products. Accordingly, approaches to diversity have changed and will continue to evolve as determined by changes in organizational structures and the economy. Underlying corporations' diversity efforts, in essence, is a *process* rather than an intervention. Hence, its outcomes are not easily determined or measured.

However, by exploring corporations' diversity structures and behaviors, what is gained here is a better understanding of how employment is organized, how women and minority job candidates are pursued, and how they are placed in and retained by organizational structure and behavior. In turn, through structural explanations of how corporations attract, hire, and retain women and minorities, this work illuminates how social inequality can persist, be resisted, and be tolerated when organizational structures shape, produce, and reproduce the changing contexts and boundaries of business organizations.

My friend Donald and I talked often during the writing of this book. Having a fair amount of experience in corporate America, he expressed his concerns regarding the issue of the global economy. He is worried about foreign investment and the national deficit. Recognizing the unsettling nature of the global marketplace, Donald posed an important question: "Who is going to own us? Does it really matter and should we care?" Later that day, I thought about our conversation and asked myself, "What does this incredibly important issue have to do with corporate diversity strategies?"

In fact, it brought back a recent experience in a local furniture store. I was shopping with my friend Sharon and we came across a lovely store where all of the furniture is made in Latin America. It's purchased in the store in Virginia and is then manufactured and shipped, over the next two and half months, to the store from Latin America. What was incredibly interesting about my shopping experience that day was how the sales gentleman provided us with a lecture on foreign investment. He shared what he considered to be very valuable information. He told us to invest only in foreign currency, to invest only in funding sources overseas. This would eventually be very profitable for us.

Again, I pose the question: What does this have to do with corporations' efforts to attract and retain women and minorities? I guess probably not a whole lot in the grand scheme of things. Economic issues such as foreign investment, global markets, profits, and international trade do not compare to minor issues of underlying diversity. But recent data from the U.S. Census Bureau claim that by 2043, the United States will be minority in the majority, with Latinos composing the largest segment of the nation's population.

The future of emerging populations, not emerging markets, concerns me most. The welfare and well-being of women, African Americans, Latinos, Native Americans, and Asians are critical at this juncture in American history. Soon, their overwhelming presence will shift focus in our American institutions. No doubt, corporations in particular will shape that focus. It is my hope that this work somehow anticipates how institutions will continue to manage diverse populations. By doing so, I trust that a brighter future of economic mobility and unique opportunities will exist for the new majority and that their experiences will be found in the American dream. A dream emphasized in 1953 by Thomas J. Watson, Jr., first president of International Business Machines Corporation.

INTERNATIONAL BUSINESS MACHINES CORPORATION
500 MADISON AVENUE
NEW YORK 22, NY

OFFICE OF   September 21, 1953
THE PRESIDENT
Confidential

Policy Letter #4

The purpose of this letter is to restate for all of the supervisory personnel of the IBM Company the policy of this corporation regarding the hiring of personnel with specific reference to race, color, or creed.

Under the American system, each of the citizens of this country has an equal right to live and work in America. It is the policy of this organization to hire people who have the personality, talent and background necessary to fill a given job, regardless of race, color or creed.

If everyone in IBM who hires new employees will observe this rule, the corporation will obtain the type of people it requires, and at the same time we will be affording an equal opportunity to all in accordance with American tradition.

T. J. Watson, Jr.

T. J. Watson, Jr.

Research Method

T he following research questions and hypotheses were created to determine why and how information technology (IT) corporations adopt and implement diversity strategies. A detailed discussion of measurement follows. It is important to understand the methodological approach to this study in order to gain a broader picture of data-collection methods.

Research Questions and Hypotheses

Question 1: Do interorganizational ties with external organizations affect the adoption of diversity strategies?

Hypothesis 1: IT corporations most likely to adopt diversity strategies maintain active and effective ties with influential organizations such as women and minority science and engineering organizations, women- and minority-serving colleges and universities, women and minority professional and community groups, the K–12 education system, women and minority career magazines and journals, and the U.S. military. This hypothesis suggests that interorganizational ties between IT corporations and women- and minority-targeted IT-related organizations and education institutions exist for the allocation and procurement of resources such as women and minority personnel, public approval, and political advocacy (Galaskiewicz 1985).

Question 2: Do legal mandates and political pressures affect the adoption of diversity strategies?

Hypothesis 2: Under conditions of legal mandates and political pressures, corporations are more likely to adopt diversity strategies. In the spirit of DiMaggio and Powell's (1983) work, the state exerts coercive pressure on organizations to adapt their structures and activities to institutionalized norms. This hypothesis suggests that federal and state employment laws, government contracts, and political organizations' statements on immigration policies (H-1B visas) affect the adoption of diversity strategies.

Question 3a: Does the proportion of women and minority human resources professionals affect the adoption of diversity strategies?

Hypothesis 3a: IT corporations that employ a higher proportion of women and minority human resources professionals are more likely to adopt diversity strategies than those who do not.

Question 3b: Does the presence of a female or minority human resources manager affect the adoption of diversity strategies?

Hypothesis 3b: Corporations that employ a female or minority human resources manager are more likely to adopt diversity strategies.

Hypotheses 3a and 3b suggest that professionals often determine corporate responses to unclear legal mandates (Edelman 1992; Sutton and Dobbin 1996). Because human resources professionals are often in charge of and monitor civil rights and equal employment opportunity policies (Kelly and Dobbin 1999), it stands to reason that they are most likely to motivate and encourage the adoption of diversity strategies.

Question 4: Do bureaucratic control practices affect the adoption of diversity strategies?

Hypothesis 4: IT corporations with bureaucratic control practices are more likely to adopt diversity strategies. This hypothesis rests on the principle of bureaucratic control (Edwards 1979). In this context, firms that adopt diversity strategies are more likely to implement hiring, training, and retention programs and activities to recruit and retain women and minority IT professionals.

Question 5: Do firm age and firm size affect the adoption of diversity strategies? This question derives from the research of Kelly and Dobbin (1999) and their hypotheses concerning the firm's adoption of maternity leave policies and Edelman's study on legal ambiguity and symbolic structures. The same question and hypotheses are posed in this study regarding firm age and firm size given their applicability and relevance to this research study.

Hypothesis 5a: Older corporations are more likely to adopt diversity strategies. This hypothesis suggests that older companies are less likely to be resistant to change and more likely to adopt new strategies. This expectation challenges the work of Salancik (1957) and Stinchcombe (1965), indicating that organizations have difficulty changing or reinventing established practices.

Hypothesis 5b: Larger corporations are more likely to adopt diversity strategies. In her study, Edelman (1992) suggests that larger companies were likely to be highly visible. Because of the visibility, larger corporations are more likely to be targeted by enforcement agencies and the increase of legal sanctions encourages corporations to implement affirmative action structures. Edelman (1992) also points out that larger corporations enjoy economics of scale; they can easily allocate resources for EEO/AA structures. Accordingly, I expect that larger IT corporations are more likely to adopt diversity strategies than small and mid-sized corporations.

Measurement

Dependent Variable. The dependent variable in this study is *formalized diversity strategies*. Specifically, survey informants (respondents) were asked whether or not their organization had a *written* policy or mission statement on diversity. Informants were asked to provide a printed copy of their written diversity statement or print the statement in the space allocated in the survey questionnaire. Informants indicating "we do not have one" or "NA" or who chose to leave the space blank were considered as "having no diversity strategies." For those informants who provided a copy or printed version of their diversity statement, they were defined as "adopting diversity strategies." Because the questionnaire did not investigate the extent of a firm's implementation of diversity strategies, I considered only the actual written diversity statement as an indication of the adoption of diversity strategies. As Beyer and Trice (1978) suggest, if a policy (strategy) has been implemented at all, it must first have been adopted, and if it is to be adopted, it first has to be written down.

Independent Variables. The independent variables attempt to predict influence of the adoption of diversity strategies. The following are the independent variables:

Organizational Ties. The measures of organizational ties were chosen by examination of businesses' written materials on employment—recruitment, hiring, training, and the retention of women and minorities.

Using a Likert-scale of 0 to 5, informants were asked to what extent were the following organizational affiliations effective in successfully recruiting women and minorities: partnerships with K–12 school systems, women- and minority-serving colleges and universities, serving on a college or university governance board, collaboration with the U.S. military, hosting receptions for women and minority organizations, participating in women and minority career fairs, and implementing school-to-work transition programs.

Control Variables. Like other important studies, control variables employed in this dissertation illustrate theoretically relevant variables as indicators of the adoption of nondiscrimination policies and practices (Baron et al. 1991; Dobbin et al. 1993; Edelman 1992). Control variables include firm characteristics such as revenue volume, firm type, and regional location. Revenue volume referred to the yearly income reported

questionnaire. The number of employees within three numerical ranges—200 to 499, 500 to 999, and 1,000+—served as measures of firm size. Information on firm size was gathered prior to the dissemination of the survey questionnaire and was obtained from a guide to U.S. business and industry, the *Dun & Bradstreet Executive Title Directory.*

Research Steps and Procedures

I began gathering data on why and how information technology corporations adopt diversity strategies by identifying information technology intensive corporations in the United States. The sample frame for this study is the *Dun & Bradstreet Executive Title Directory.* This directory is appropriate for this research given its comprehensive inclusion of business and industry throughout the country. Corporations were selected based on U.S. Standard Industry Classifications (SIC) codes. Corporations' names, addresses, and phone numbers were provided by Survey Sampling, Incorporated, a reputable research firm located in the Northeast. A total of six hundred firms were selected randomly. In order to ensure a broad representative sample, the number of IT firms was of equal proportion in three employee size categories (200 to 499, 500 to 999, and 1000+). For additional analysis, firms were also identified by revenue volume, regional location, and age.

Guided by Dillman's (2001) *Mail and Internet Surveys: The Tailored Design Method,* self-administered questionnaires were mailed to human resources professionals employed within randomly selected IT corporations. Human resources professionals are the most appropriate informants for this study, given their knowledge of and responsibility for managing and operating a range of activities, programs, and operations concerning the recruitment, hiring, training, and retention of employees. Many organizational studies investigating the various and multiple aspects of employment tend to draw upon the presence, experiences, behaviors, opinions, and attitudes of human resources professionals.

Instrument. The survey questionnaire examined informants' reports on the recruiting, hiring, training, and retention activities adopted to employ and retain U.S.-born women and minorities, namely African Americans, Asian Americans, Latinos, and Native Americans. It was necessary to create questions that would encourage informants to begin and continue to the end. In this regard, questions were presented in an order of sequence to ensure a sense of logic and clear understanding of the purpose of the study. To provide consistency throughout the questionnaire, the format of closed-ended questions with ordered-answer choices was employed to address anticipated time constraints of informants. Dillman (2001) suggests that this format can yield concise, usable, and cost-effective responses. A few open-ended important questions were included in the questionnaire, such as "What is your company's statement on diversity?" and "What is your company's age?"

After pre-testing the instrument several times, one interesting outcome of pre-testing suggested that the language "IT firms" used in the letter of introduction and on the front cover of the questionnaire created confusion. Some firms declined to participate because they did not identify as an "IT firm" but they did employ a large number of "IT professionals." In response to this confusion, to provide clarification as to what types of firms would be eligible for participation in the study, the language "IT firms" was changed to read "IT employers" in hopes of including a broad range of firms that define themselves exclusively as "manufacturers," "developers," "trainers," "producers," and "appliers" of information technologies.

In addition, pre-testing ensured that all pertinent aspects of recruitment, hiring, training, and retention strategies were included and appropriately addressed and presented in the questionnaire. Individual survey items were grouped into categories addressing the study's primary areas of interest—recruitment, hiring, training, and retention.

To avoid holiday mail traffic, the first wave of questionnaires was mailed to firms in early November. Four to five weeks following the first mailing, a reminder/thank you postcard was mailed to all informants. Based on Dillman's (2001) finding that such a strategy will increase the response rate by 20 to 40 percent, a careful follow-up sequence was initiated. It is important to note here that the *timing* of the questionnaires' dissemination was problematic. In the midst of distribution, the U.S. Postal Service's processing and delivery operations were interrupted by mail contamination of anthrax. Consequently, the U.S. Postal Service's processes and procedures for handling every form of mail were altered, resulting in significant delays, errors, and lost items. Moreover, given the demonstrated fatal effects of anthrax, many organizations limited their receipt of mail correspondence determined not to be relevant or familiar to their day-to-day business operations.

Striving to increase the response rate, after eliminating firms who had completed and returned the questionnaire, firms who declined to participate or were ineligible, and firms whose addresses were not correct or no longer in existence, two additional mail contacts were made involving a reminder letter, replacement questionnaire, and a glow-in-the-dark light bulb magnet with a personalized inscription, which served as a reminder as well as a token of appreciation. After a period of four months, I began to telephone a select number of IT corporations and request their participation in my study. By personally reminding informants to complete and return the questionnaire, I found that informants were more apt to return the questionnaire within several days. Due to significant cost constraints and time limits, I ended the ten-month period of data collection involving the survey questionnaire.

Response Rate. Survey questionnaires were mailed to exactly six hundred IT corporations across the United States. To ensure representativeness of the survey population, the sample was divided into three categories by firm size—200–499, 500–999, and 1000+ employees. Within each firm-size category, an equal number (two hundred) of questionnaires were mailed. The response rate was calculated "as the percentage of eligible informants that result in completed interviews or questionnaires" (Dillman 1978, 2001).

In order to qualify as an eligible respondent, a firm must have been contactable by both mail and telephone. In this study, there were *one hundred* completed questionnaires out of a total of five hundred thirty-five eligible IT firms (contactable both by mail and telephone), yielding an adjusted response rate of 44 percent.[4]

Although not desirable, the 54 percent response rate yielded in this study was quite favorable compared to similar published and scholarly organization studies. In some cases, the response rate yielded in this study was higher: Blau et al. (1976) yielded a response rate of 36 percent, Lincoln and Kalleberg (1985) reported a completion rate of 35 percent, Edelman (1992) reported a response rate of 54 percent, and Dobbin and

Sutton (1998) reported a response rate of 45 percent. In general, the literature on organization studies notes the difficulty of obtaining high response rates. Pennings (1973) argues:

> Because the subject matter of the scales deals with the perception of structural properties of organizations rather than with attitudes, opinions or feelings, response rates probably affect possible distortions to a much smaller extent than do refusal rates in research on attitudes and opinion, where systematic biases may be strongly associated with the very attitudes that are measured.

IT corporations that "declined" to participate indicated many reasons: time constraints, unavailability of the information required for the survey, limited human resources to complete the questionnaire, and being in the process of developing or revising diversity strategies, and corporate policy prohibited participation in the study. IT corporations that indicated they were "not eligible" provided three reasons: they employed an inadequate number of women and minority IT professionals, a cessation of recruiting and hiring employees or current laying off of a significant number of employees, and a cessation of employing IT professionals due to contracting with other organizations for IT personnel.

Given the consistently changing nature of information technology and the state of the U.S. economy at the time of this study, it was not surprising that a fair proportion of the potential survey participants (10 percent) no longer existed or had recently entered into mergers, alliances, or takeovers. Several follow-up phone inquiries provided evidence that IT corporations that were "not contactable" were no longer in operation or were being acquired by other corporations.

Nonresponse Bias Analysis. This study attempted to survey a nationally representative sample of six hundred IT businesses. One hundred IT corporations completed and returned survey questionnaires (yielding an adjusted response rate of 54 percent). I conducted a nonresponse bias analysis to address concerns of whether or not certain subgroups of the IT sector were excluded from the analysis. In this regard, it is crucial to determine if certain subgroups within the IT sector, such as smaller, younger, and less profitable firms, were less likely to respond. Implications of nonresponse bias would affect this study's internal validity and external generalizability.

In order to assess the likelihood that the results may be biased because of nonresponse to the survey questionnaire, I randomly selected fifteen IT corporations, five within each firm-size category, which did not participate in the study. This process was difficult given that there was record of actual contact names associated with each IT company. After three weeks, contact was established with the human resources manager who actually recalled receiving the survey questionnaire. Over the telephone, I asked if they would explain why they did not return the questionnaire and whether or not they would agree to answer a reduced subset of questions from each questionnaire category. Ten questions considered to be most relevant to possible explanations of why and how IT firms adopt diversity strategies were asked of each person. In most cases, informants were very cooperative and answered questions at the time of the initial telephone call. Fewer than six required scheduling appointments in advance.

The nonresponse analysis suggests that nonrespondents and respondents differ in two particular systemic ways—firm size and adoption of diversity strategies. As anticipated, nonrespondents were more likely to be smaller firms. In fact, of all nonrespondents, 47 percent were small firms (200–499). The nonresponse bias analysis also indicated that nonrespondents, primarily small firms, were more likely *not* to have adopted formal, well-articulated diversity statements. This study's findings are generalizable to *large* IT corporations who *adopt* diversity strategies, rather than smaller firms without diversity statements.

Given the importance of legal mandates and political pressures on equal opportunity employment practices, included in the nonresponse bias analysis were two key questions from the survey questionnaire: (1) How would you rate the impact of federal policies such as EEO/AA on your company's recruiting and hiring practices? (2) To what extent has your company responded to changes in Affirmative Action directives? Results show that noninformants were twice as likely as informants to report "a little" to question 1 and "a little" to question 2. This finding suggests that nonrespondents may be more conservative in their perceptions of the importance of federal policies on the firm's employment practices.

Hence, they may not have been motivated to participate in a survey focused on corporate diversity strategies.

Because half of the targeted population completed and returned survey questionnaires, a nonresponse bias analysis was required. Data presented in this study are affected by nonresponse and, as anticipated, the results presented in the subsequent chapters are not generalizable to all corporations in the IT sector, but rather to larger firms (1,000 or more employees) that tend to have formal, well-articulated statements on diversity. These corporations usually highly visible, well-known, and under pressure to enforce federal policies such as Equal Employment Opportunity and Affirmative Action.

In testing the hypotheses posed in this study, a series of preliminary analyses were conducted to determine the strength of relationships among variables. Preliminary data analyses began with simple descriptive statistics—frequency distributions and cross-tabulations. For each questionnaire item, frequency distributions were examined to obtain a description of informants' responses. Results of the frequency distributions were striking. For the majority of survey questions, over 50 percent of the informants indicated "0," which was coded "NA" or not applicable among Likert-scale responses. Employing a scale ranging from 0 to 5 (0 coded as "NA" to 5 coded as "very effective"), the Likert-scale response categories were designed to determine the *extent* to which a program, activity, or practice affected the adoption of diversity strategies. In the case of informants reporting "NA," this meant that their company had no such program, activity, or practice; it simply did not exist within the corporation.

The high proportion of informants who reported "NA" to a large number of survey questions consequently resulted in a small number of responses across the remaining five response categories (1 to 5). To address this skewness, response categories assessing degree of effectiveness, importance, difficulty, and agreement (5 coded as "extremely," 4 coded as "very much," 3 coded as "somewhat," 2 coded as "a little," and 1 coded as "not at all") were collapsed into the two categories "no " and "yes" ("no" coded as 0 and "yes" coded as 1). To establish consistency across all questionnaire items, all Likert-scale response categories were re-coded into "yes" and "no" responses (response categories 1 to 5 were combined and re-coded as "yes" and response category 0 was re-coded as "no"). Clearly, because the data were re-coded into two categories, the original intention of the survey design was changed. Initially, the survey was designed to examine responses associated with the *extent* to which corporations adopted specific diversity strategies. However, preliminary analysis suggested a slightly different picture—*whether or not* firms adopt specific diversity strategies *at all*. Hence, this picture reflects more accurately the data collected.

Because there was a small number of firms classified within a large number of Standard Industry Classification codes, twenty-three individual SIC codes were combined into five broader SIC code categories for the purpose of comparison and analysis. Five categories were created based on the similarity of industry type and the method of production of information technologies.

Other important preliminary data analyses were conducted to determine the best and most appropriate statistical techniques in analyzing the survey data. For example, to determine the strength of the association between two variables, Pearson's correlation coefficients were examined. To determine what factors were significantly related to the adoption of diversity strategies, chi-square tests were conducted. Further, as a means of classifying a number of interrelated variables such as race and gender of informants, proportion of women and minority IT professionals, and proportion of women and minority human resources professionals, a factor analysis was conducted to identify possible underlying associations or indicators.

Guided by Whyte's key informant interview method (1985), interview questions were created to cover all relevant areas of interest in one interview. The first concern of the interview process was to reassure the respondent that our conversation would be kept completely confidential and that in no way would the study identify them by name or would their name be linked to their employer. As indicated in the letter of introduction, I reminded each informant that University policies existed to ensure their confidentiality and the anonymity of their corporation. In order to establish credibility by demonstrating that the interviews were conducted in a manner in which the informants were accurately identified and described (Lincoln and Guba 1985), I assured informants that they would be provided an opportunity prior to publication of the study's results to review and provide feedback on interpretations resulting from data analysis.

The first concern of the key informant interview was to establish "rapport" (Whyte 1985). To accomplish this, the first two questions asked informants to describe their work and what it details and how their work responsibilities and tasks fit within the larger corporation. Next, informants were asked a set of questions that provided them the opportunity to be reflective on significant events. Because informants can usually talk at length on a question that can be answered by a single word or phrase, interview questions were created in a *restricted* manner, that is, distinguishable as *descriptive, evaluative,* and *nonspecific questions* (Whyte 1985). I chose not to employ one specific type of question but rather a mix of restrictive questions. By doing so, I anticipated a broader and richer range of information.

The *descriptive* questions were created to capture the particulars of a specific event that occurred within a series of events. The *evaluative* questions sought to reveal how the informant *feels or felt at one time* about a situation, people, or the corporation. And, *nonspecific questions* were concerned with responses yielded from a combination of descriptive and evaluative questions.

When appropriate, certain interview strategies were employed to assist the informant to express themselves more fully on matters of concern to them. As Whyte (1985, 99) states, "In research, we want the informant to talk about things of vital interest to them, but we also need their cooperation in covering materials of importance to us that are of possible little interest to the informant." Hence, throughout the informant interviews, I used what Whyte calls the "directive" technique. The directive technique allowed me to interrupt gracefully during the interview process by stating "uh-huh" or "that's interesting." Such language simply encouraged informants to continue without exerting any influence on the direction of their responses. The *reflection* technique provided a bit more direction, implying that the informant should continue discussing the topic or situation at hand. This technique was implemented usually by repeating a last phrase or response stated by the informant but with a rising inflection. By *probing the informant's last remark,* attention was directed to the last idea expressed.

Slightly differing from the *reflection* technique, I would often raise some question or make a statement about the informant's last remark. Further, by *probing an idea* following the informant's last remark (but within the scope of the informant's last statement), the opportunity was created for the informant to express more fully many more ideas, adding to the richness of informant information. Whyte argues that it is important to go back to an earlier portion of the interview and *probe an idea* expressed by the informant. As a result of doing so, I was able to broaden my choices of topics and consequently exercise more control rather than be limited to only preceding remarks made by the informant. Lastly, by *introducing a new topic,* I was able to raise a topic that had not yet surfaced and consequently the interview process continued smoothly. Because key informant interview methodology cautions our reliance upon the human memory, all informant interviews were tape-recorded to ensure an *exact* record of questions and responses. Also in accordance, each interview tape was professionally transcribed.

To analyze interviews, this study employed five analytic procedures (Marshall and Rossman 1995). First, data were organized. Then, categories, themes, and patterns were generated. The third step comprised testing emergent hypotheses against data, and the fourth, searching for alternative explanations. Finally, writing the report concluded the analyses. Each phase of the data analyses included data reduction as a means of managing a voluminous amount of information. Also, essential to the analysis process were interpretations—whereby I bring meaning and insights to the words and acts of the informants.

By organizing the data, it was necessary to read and re-read data transcriptions in order to become familiar and intimate with the informants' words. To generate categories, themes, and patterns, I paid careful attention to recurring language, patterns of belief that link individuals and settings together, and salient themes across all interview data. To test emergent hypotheses, I searched the data for negative instances of patterns. I carefully evaluated the data for information inadequacy, credibility, usefulness, and centrality. In order to search for alternative explanations, I attempted to engage in a critical act of challenging the very pattern that was so apparent. As a result, the search for other plausible data and important linkages among them could emerge. As Marshall and Rossman (1995) argue, alternative explanations *always* exist. Finally, writing the report involved choosing particular words to summarize and reflect the complexity of the data. To summarize, this process required the act of interpreting—lending shape, form, and meaning—to a large amount of raw data.

Appendix A

Participating Corporations

1. Accu-Sort Systems, Inc
2. Advanced Digital Information Corporation
3. Advanced Resources Technologies
4. Alphanumeric Systems, Inc
5. Alpha Technologies Group
6. America Online
7. American Bechtel, Inc
8. AMS Management Systems Group, Inc
9. Arimon Technologies, Inc
10. ASMO North Carolina, Inc
11. AT&T Corporation
12. Belkin Corporation
13. Bell Labs/Lucent Technologies
14. BellSouth Corporation
15. Berliner Communications Corporation
16. Broadreach Consulting, Inc
17. Cable Express Corporation
18. CACI International Corporation
19. CGS Systems International
20. Chorum Technologies, Inc
21. Cisco Systems, Inc
22. Citicorp Data Systems, Inc
23. Clarent Corporation

24. Click Commerce, Inc
25. Comdial Corporation
26. Commerce One, Inc
27. Commonwealth Telephone Co
28. Computer Services, Inc
29. Concord Tel Long Distance, Inc
30. Creative Technologies Corporation
31. Crestron Electronics Corporation
32. Culinaire of Florida, Inc
33. Data Processing Sciences Corporation
34. Deltek Systems, Inc
35. E-Commerce Support Centers
36. EarthLink Corporation
37. EDS Corporation
38. Epitec Group
39. Epixtech, Inc
40. Evans & Sutherland Computer Corporation
41. Finetix Corporation
42. First Health Services Corporation
43. First Virtual Communications Corporation
44. Focal Communications, Inc
45. General Dynamics
46. HP Corporation
47. HNC Software, Inc
48. IBM Corporation
49. IP Communications Corporation
50. Ilex Systems
51. InFlow, Inc
52. Integic Corporation
53. Intel Corporation
54. Interbrand Corporation
55. International Fuel Cells
56. ISE Labs, Inc
57. Kronos Incorporated
58. Level 8 Systems, Inc
59. LHS Communications System
60. Library Systems & Services, Inc

61. ManTech International Corporation
62. Maxima Technologies, Inc
63. Metamor Industry Solutions
64. Microchip Technology, Inc
65. Microsoft Corporation
66. Minolta-QMS, Inc
67. Motorola Corporation
68. National Business Systems
69. National Semiconductors Corporation
70. New Era of Networks, Inc
71. Nokia Corporation
72. Novell Corporation, Inc
73. Oracle Corporation
74. Oven Digital Group, Inc
75. Paragon Solutions Corporation
76. Polaris Software Labs
77. Printronix, Inc
78. Qwest Corporation, Inc
79. SeeBeyond Technology Corporation
80. Scient Corporation
81. Sharp Laboratories of America
82. Sierra Tel Communications Group
83. Smithville Telephone Company, Inc
84. Sony PC Support Corporation
85. Sumitomo Sitix Phoenix, Inc
86. Superior Consultant Holdings Corporation
87. Systemax Manufacturing, Inc
88. Tally Holdings, Inc
89. Teksystems, Inc
90. Texas Instruments Corporation
91. Telecordia Technologies, Inc
92. Therma-Wave, Inc
93. Tripos, Inc
94. Turnstone Systems, Inc
95. Verizon Corporation
96. Verizon Data Services, Inc
97. Vis.align Corporation

Appendix B

Organizational Responses to Diversity: A Survey of the Nation's Information Technology Employers

Recruiting Strategies

1. Is your company experiencing difficulty finding qualified IT professionals? (Check one)
   _____Yes   _____No   _____Somewhat

   If **yes** or **somewhat**, please indicate how *difficult* finding qualified IT professionals is for your company, using the following scale: (Circle one)

Not at all Difficult (1)	A little difficult (2)	Somewhat difficult (3)	Very much difficult (4)	Extremely difficult (5)

2. Is your company experiencing difficulty finding qualified women and minority IT professionals? (Check one)
   _____Yes   _____No   _____Sometimes

   If **yes** or **somewhat**, please indicate how *difficult* finding qualified women and minority IT professionals is for your company, using the following scale: (Circle one)

Not at all difficult (1)	A little difficult (2)	Somewhat difficult (3)	Very much difficult (4)	Extremely difficult (5)

3. Of your women and minority IT professionals, estimate the percentage that received long-term educational and professional training (e.g., renewed licenses, degrees, certificates) from your company? (Circle one)

   0–25%   26%–50%   51%–75%   76%–100%

4. To what extent has your company found women and minorities without IT professional credentials, but with potential? (Circle one)

Not at all (1)	A little (2)	Somewhat (3)	Very much (4)	Extremely (5)

5. To what extent does your company recruit lesser-qualified women and minorities and develop them internally? (Circle one)

Not at all (1)	A little (2)	Somewhat (3)	Very much (4)	Extremely (5)

6. Please identify the specific jobs that your company has the *most* difficulty finding women and minority talent for (e.g., programmers, analysts, engineers, etc.):

_____

_____

7. Does your company require that professional staff have at least a bachelor's degree in an IT-related discipline? (Check one)

_____Yes   _____No

8. Do most of your women and minority employees have at least a bachelor's degree in an IT-related discipline? (Check one)

_____Yes   _____No

9. To what extent does your company agree that the supply of women and minority IT talent is a problem originating from the K–12 and higher education systems?

Not at all	A little	Somewhat	Very much	Extremely
(1)	(2)	(3)	(4)	(5)

10. To what extent would your company rate the effectiveness of K-12 education in preparing future women and minority IT professionals?

N/A	Not at all effective	A little effective	Somewhat effective	Very much effective	Extremely effective
(0)	(1)	(2)	(3)	(4)	(5)

11. To what extent would your company rate the effectiveness of colleges and universities in preparing future women and minority IT professionals?

N/A	Not at all effective	A little effective	Somewhat effective	Very much effective	Extremely effective
(0)	(1)	(2)	(3)	(4)	(5)

12. How would your company rate the effectiveness of college and university programs (e.g., computer science, computer engineering, electrical engineering) in preparing IT women and minority students for work/careers in IT?

N/A	Not at all effective	A little effective	Somewhat effective	Very much effective	Extremely effective
(0)	(1)	(2)	(3)	(4)	(5)

13. To what extent does your company recruit and hire women and minority job seekers who are not students?

Not at all	A little	Somewhat	Very much	Extremely
(1)	(2)	(3)	(4)	(5)

14. To what extent has your company been successful at recruiting women and minority job seekers who are not students?

Not at all	A little	Somewhat	Very much	Extremely
(1)	(2)	(3)	(4)	(5)

15. How would you rate the level of IT skills among most non-student women and minorities in the labor pool?

_____Poor _____Satisfactory _____Very Good _____Excellent

16. To what extent is prior IT work experience important in the hiring of women and minorities who are not students within your company?

Not at all	A little	Somewhat	Very much	Extremely
(1)	(2)	(3)	(4)	(5)

17. Normally, are most women and minority (non-students) job candidates recruited from other firms for employment within your company?

_____Yes _____No _____Sometimes

18. Does your company provide incentives to senior managers (e.g., bonuses) for the successful recruitment and hiring of women and minority IT professionals?

_____Yes _____No

Provided is a list of recruitment methods used for recruiting and attracting prospective employees. Please indicate how effective the following methods have been for your organization in recruiting and attracting women and minority *students*. Please use the following scale (please circle):

N/A (0)	Not at all effective (1)	A little effective (2)	Somewhat effective (3)	Very much effective (4)	Extremely effective (5)

Method	Effectiveness					
1. Local K–12 school partnerships	0	1	2	3	4	5
2. Hosting receptions and dinners targeted toward women and minorities on campus	0	1	2	3	4	5
3. Sponsoring workshops targeted toward women and minorities on campus	0	1	2	3	4	5
4. Offering special scholarships and fellowships for women and minority students	0	1	2	3	4	5
5. Participating in women and minority career fairs on campus	0	1	2	3	4	5
6. Advertising in women- and minority-targeted career magazines	0	1	2	3	4	5
7. Sponsoring women and minority internship/co-opt programs	0	1	2	3	4	5
8. Targeting colleges with women and minority populations (e.g., HBCU, HACU[1], Women's Colleges)	0	1	2	3	4	5
9. Personal referrals from faculty members	0	1	2	3	4	5
10. Personal referrals from current employees	0	1	2	3	4	5
11. Referrals from key women and minority players in the corporate/government sector	0	1	2	3	4	5
12. Advertising on women- and minority-targeted campus websites, radio, or in newspapers, bulletin boards, etc.	0	1	2	3	4	5
13. Serving on college governance boards (e.g., boards of trustees, directors, etc.).	0	1	2	3	4	5
14. Transition programs from college to work	0	1	2	3	4	5

Note: [1] Item 8: HBCU=Historically Black Colleges & Universities; Hispanic Association of Colleges & Universities

Please list three colleges and universities from which your company tends to recruit women and minority employees.

_____

_____

_____

Provided is a list of recruitment methods used for recruiting and attracting prospective employees. Please indicate how effective the following methods have been for your organization in recruiting and attracting *non-student* women and minority candidates. Please use the following scale (please circle):

N/A (0)	Not at all effective (1)	A little effective (2)	Somewhat effective (3)	Very much effective (4)	Extremely effective (5)

Method	Effectiveness					
1. Hosting receptions & dinners targeting women and minorities through women and minority professional organizations and associations	0	1	2	3	4	5
2. Sponsoring and conducting workshops at women and minority professional meetings	0	1	2	3	4	5
3. Establishing substantive relationships with women and minority nonprofit organizations & associations (financial contributors)	0	1	2	3	4	5
4. Advertising in women and minority magazines, on websites, newspapers, etc.	0	1	2	3	4	5
5. Personal referrals from key women and minority players in the corporate sector	0	1	2	3	4	5
6. Personal referrals from current employees	0	1	2	3	4	5
7. Participation with local women and minority community groups	0	1	2	3	4	5
8. Establishing special training programs with other organizations targeted toward women and minorities	0	1	2	3	4	5
9. Working collaboratively with the U.S. military branches	0	1	2	3	4	5
10. Serving on women and minority professional organizations' governance boards (e.g., board of directors, governing councils, etc.)	0	1	2	3	4	5
11. Target women and minority science and engineering professional organizations, such as the Associations of Black, Hispanic and Native American Scientists and Engineers	0	1	2	3	4	5
12. Contracting with headhunting firms	0	1	2	3	4	5

From the list below, please indicate the top 3 reasons why your company participates or utilizes some of the recruitment methods and strategies listed above.

_____ CEO/president is strongly committed to diversity
_____ Diversity is a strategic objective of the company
_____ Diversity is a good business imperative; buying power of women and minorities
_____ Diversity is a moral/social imperative
_____ Other companies are doing it
_____ Mandated by government policies   _____ Improves customer/client relationships
_____ Pressure from customers/clients   _____ Stockholders' commitment to diversity
_____ Trendy, latest organizational fad   _____ Other (please specify)

2. Hiring Practices

1. What is your company's specific mission/strategy statement concerning diversity?
   _____
   _____
   _____

2. Please rate the impact of federal policies, such as Equal Opportunity, Affirmative Action, non-discrimination, and other policies on your company's recruiting and hiring practices. (Circle one)

Not at all effective	A little effective	Somewhat effective	Very much effective	Extremely effective
(1)	(2)	(3)	(4)	(5)

3. To what extent has your company responded to changes in Affirmative Action/EEO directives?

Not at all	A little	Some	A lot	Extremely
(1)	(2)	(3)	(4)	(5)

4. Has your company responded to any new court judgments regarding hiring practices of women and minorities, such as class action suits?   Yes   No

5. Does your company monitor and evaluate its recruitment and hiring practices concerning women and minorities?   Yes   No   Sometimes

6. In your recruiting process, does your company offer special incentives to women and minorities (for example, bonuses, fringe benefits, flex-time, travel, sabbaticals, etc.)?   Yes   No   Sometimes

7. To what extent does your company participate with state and local government (e.g., contracts, agreements) for the hiring of women and minorities?

Not at all	A little	Some	A lot	Extremely
(1)	(2)	(3)	(4)	(5)

8. To what extent is your company aware of national and political organizations' (e.g., National Urban League, Congressional Black Caucus) statements against immigrant policies (e.g., visas) concerning employment in the IT industry?

Not at all	A little	Some	A lot	Extremely
(1)	(2)	(3)	(4)	(5)

9. To what extent does your company agree that immigration policies impact the hiring of women and minorities in IT?

Not at all	A little	Some	A lot	Extremely
(1)	(2)	(3)	(4)	(5)

3. Training Strategies

Below are a few questions concerning your company's training and staff development progress. Please answer the questions using the following scale:

Not at all	A little	Some	A lot	Extremely
(1)	(2)	(3)	(4)	(5)

1. To what extent does your company provide training for women and minority IT professionals?   1   2   3   4   5

2. How often does your company rely on four-year colleges/universities for the training of your employees?   1   2   3   4   5

3. To what extent does your company contract for external training programs for women and minorities?   1   2   3   4   5

4. Of your women and minority new hires, what percent normally require training? (Circle one)

   0–25%   26%–50%   51%–75%   76%–100%

4. Retention Strategies

Provided is a list of formal and informal retention programs. Please indicate the effectiveness of the program or activity for your organization in retaining women and minority employees, using the following scale:

N/A (0)	Not at all effective (1)	A little effective (2)	Somewhat effective (3)	Very much effective (4)	Extremely effective (5)

Formal Program	Effectiveness					
Executive Leadership Program	0	1	2	3	4	5
Rotating Job Assignment Program	0	1	2	3	4	5
Work Assignments across the Company	0	1	2	3	4	5
Supervisory/Annual Review Program	0	1	2	3	4	5
Incentives (financial, promotions, etc.)	0	1	2	3	4	5
Succession Plans	0	1	2	3	4	5
Continuing Education Programs	0	1	2	3	4	5
Professional Training Programs	0	1	2	3	4	5
Informal Program	**Effectiveness**					
Mentoring Programs	0	1	2	3	4	5
Support Groups (e.g., Black Caucus)	0	1	2	3	4	5
Job Training for Specific Assignments	0	1	2	3	4	5
Employee Recognition Programs	0	1	2	3	4	5
Internal Newsletters/Publications	0	1	2	3	4	5
Workshops/Seminars on Networking and Communications	0	1	2	3	4	5
Work/Life Programs (designed to help employees balance work and family)	0	1	2	3	4	5

5. Company Profile

Profile of Women and Minorities
Please estimate the percentage of women and minorities employed by your company who are U.S. citizens, in specific.

	Percentage (%)
African American	_____
Asian	_____
Hispanic/Latino)	_____
Native American	_____
Women	_____

What percentage of your company's HR/Personnel Department is minority? (Circle one)

     0–25%   26%–50%   51%–75%   76%–100%

What percentage of your company's HR/Personnel Department are women? (Circle one)

     0–25%   26%–50%   51%–75%   76%–100%

Please list any company awards or recognitions earned for demonstrated leadership and excellence for diversity in the workplace.

_____

_____

Please indicate the age of your company.   _____

Please indicate if your company is publicly traded. _____Yes _____No

Please indicate what best describes your company's revenue volume for 2001.
- _____ Less than 1 million
- _____ 1 million–25 million
- _____ 25 million–75 million
- _____ 75 million–200 million
- _____ 200 million–500-million
- _____ 500 million–1 billion
- _____ Over 1 billion

Provided is a list of Women and Minority Science and Engineering Organizations. Please indicate the effectiveness of your membership in these organizations for recruiting prospective women and minority employees to your company. Please use the following scale:

N/A (0)	Not at all effective (1)	A little effective (2)	Somewhat effective (3)	Very much effective (4)	Extremely effective (5)

Women and Minority Science and Engineering Organization	Effectiveness					
American Association of Women Entrepreneurs	0	1	2	3	4	5
American Indian Science & Engineering Society	0	1	2	3	4	5
Association for Puerto Ricans in Science & Engineering	0	1	2	3	4	5
Association of Muslim Scientists & Engineers	0	1	2	3	4	5
Association for Women in Science (AWIS)	0	1	2	3	4	5
Black Data Processing Association	0	1	2	3	4	5
Black Engineer.com	0	1	2	3	4	5
Black Geeks Online	0	1	2	3	4	5
Catalyst	0	1	2	3	4	5
Chinese Software Professionals Association	0	1	2	3	4	5
Institute for Women and Technology (IWT)	0	1	2	3	4	5
Korean American Scientists and Engineers Association	0	1	2	3	4	5
Mexican American Engineers and Scientists Society (MAES)	0	1	2	3	4	5
Minority Science and Engineering Program	0	1	2	3	4	5
Native Americans in Science	0	1	2	3	4	5
National Action Council on Minorities in Engineering	0	1	2	3	4	5
National Association for Minority Engineering Program Administrators	0	1	2	3	4	5
National Association of Mathematicians (NAM)	0	1	2	3	4	5
National Association of Minority Engineering Administrators	0	1	2	3	4	5
National Council of Black Scientists and Engineers (NCBES)	0	1	2	3	4	5
National Network of Minority Women in Science	0	1	2	3	4	5
National Society of Black Engineers (NSBE)	0	1	2	3	4	5
National Technical Association	0	1	2	3	4	5
Society for the Advancement of Chicanos & Native American Science	0	1	2	3	4	5
Society for Hispanic Professional Engineers and Scientists (SHPES)	0	1	2	3	4	5
National Society of Hispanic Professional Engineers (NSHPE)	0	1	2	3	4	5
Society of Mexican American Engineers & Scientists (SMAES)	0	1	2	3	4	5
Society of Women Engineers (SWE)	0	1	2	3	4	5
Southeastern Consortium for Minorities in Engineering (SECME)	0	1	2	3	4	5
Women in Engineering Programs and Advocates Network (WEPAN)	0	1	2	3	4	5
Women in Technology (WIT)	0	1	2	3	4	5
Other (please specify)_____	0	1	2	3	4	5

6. Background Information

1. What is your age? _____

2. What is your gender? _____Female _____Male

3. What is your ethnic/racial background?
   _____Asian/Pacific Islander
   _____Black/African American
   _____Hispanic
   _____Native American
   _____White
   _____Other (Please specify: _____)

4. What is your highest level of education? _____

5. What prior positions have you held? _____
   _____

6. What college have you attended? _____
   _____

_____ Yes, I would like a copy of the results of this survey. Please forward the report to the address you currently have on file.

Identifier # _____

Appendix C

Executives and Senior Managers Interview Protocol

I would like to thank you so very much for taking the time to talk with me about your work and experiences. Would you mind if I tape-record our conversation? I am very bad at taking notes while having a conversation. Okay? Shall we begin?

Work History

In general, what does your work entail at (name of firm)? How long have you been with (name of firm)? And what about in your current position?

What specific tasks does your position require of you (e.g., travel, decision making, recruiting, negotiating, strategic planning)?

Recruiting Diversity

Do you have difficulty successfully recruiting women and minority IT professionals ("IT professionals" meaning those with specialized skills in computer-based technology).

What are the reasons for the difficulty?

At (name of firm), do other departments or divisions do their own recruiting informally? If so, does this make it difficult for your office to do diversity recruitment?

Does (name of firm) tend to recruit and hire a lot of foreign-born workers? If so, does this hurt the prospects of hiring U.S.-born women and minorities?

What strategies have been used by (name of firm) to recruit women and minorities? Here is a list of typical strategies. Which ones have worked best?

a. Personal referrals	b. Providing scholarships
c. Targeting	d. Hosting campus receptions
e. Internship programs	f. Participation with local women/ minority groups
g. Advertising	h. Participation with national women/ minority groups

Does (name of firm) recruit women and minorities from historically black colleges or Hispanic-serving colleges and universities, like Howard University, North Carolina A&T, Florida A&M?

Does (name of firm) have a large number of ties or partnerships with any of these colleges?

Has (name of firm) had any particularly good experiences with certain ones? If so, could you describe them?

Are American colleges and universities producing an adequate number of well-trained, qualified women and minority IT professionals? If not, why do you think they are not being successful?

Has the applicant pool of college graduates been mostly foreign born?
If so, does this pose any difficulties, given your efforts at incorporating U.S.-born women and minorities?

Are colleges not "producing" enough women/minorities with IT skills?

Are their skills inadequate?

Retaining Diversity

What is the driving force of (name of firm) commitment to diversity?

Is it the corporate leadership—for example, the CEO, VP for HR?

Is it your clients or customers?

What have been the constraints to incorporating diversity at (name of firm)?

What strategies have been used to retain women and minorities at (name of firm?) Here is a list of typical strategies. Which ones tend to work best?

a. Support groups   b. Mentoring programs
c. Leadership programs   d. Training programs
e. Financial incentives   f. Benefits packages
g. child care programs

How important have organizations been, such as the National Association of Black Engineers and the Association of Women in Science, to incorporating diversity at (name of firm)?

Could you provide an example of how (name of firm) works collaboratively with these organizations?

What have been the *most common* reasons why women and minorities decide to leave your company?

Hiring Diversity

Does your company distinguish between Affirmative Action and EEO and diversity? If so, how?

How important have federal policies, such as EEO/AA, been on hiring women and minorities?

Can you recall an example of when, and under what circumstances, such federal policies were important?

What have been the legal or court judgments concerning incorporating diversity at (name of firm)?

Do blacks, women, and other minorities in your company tend to caucus, file complaints, and offer insight into how to handle controversial diversity-related issues?

If so, what has been the impact of their involvement?

Key Informant Information

In order to get a better sense of who you are, would you please provide me with a copy of your résumé or biography?

Bibliography

Aldrich, H. and J. Pfeffer. "Environments of Organizations." *Annual Review of Sociology* 2, (1976): 79–105.

Atkins, B. "Is Corporate Social Responsibility Responsible?" *Stanford University Innovation Review*, (2006): 33.

Baron, J. N., F. Dobbins, and P. D. Jennings. "War and Peace: The Evolution of Modern Personnel Administration in U. S. Industry." *American Journal of Sociology* 92, (1986): 350–383.

Baron, J. N., B. S. Mittman, and A. E. Newman. "Targets of Opportunity: Organizational and Environmental Determinants of Gender Integration within the California Civil Services, 1979–1985." *American Journal of Sociology* 966, (1991): 1362–1401.

Bayer, J. M. and Trice, H. M. *Implementing Change*. New York: The Free Press, 1978.

Blau, P. "Formal Organization: Dimensions of Analysis." *American Journal of Sociology* 63, (1957): 58–69.

Chandler, A. D. *Strategy and Structure*. Cambridge, MA: MIT Press, 1962.

Child, J. "Organizational Structure, Environment, and Performance: The Role of Strategic Choice." *Sociology* 6, (1972): 1–22.

Collins, S. M. *Black Corporate Executives: The Making and Breaking of a Black Middle Class*. Philadelphia: Temple University Press, 1997.

Dillman, D. *Mail and Internet Surveys: The Tailored Design Method*. New York: John Wiley and Sons, Inc., 2001.

DiMaggio, P. J. and W. W. Powell. "The Cage Revisited: Institutional Isomorphism and Collective Rationality in Organizational Fields." *American Sociological Review* 48, (1983): 147–160.

Dobbin, F. and J. Sutton. "The Strength of a Weak State: The Rights Revolution and the Rise of Human Resources Management Divisions." *American Journal of Sociology* 2, (1998): 441–476.

Dobbin, F., J. Sutton, J. Meyer, and W. R. Scott. "Equal Opportunity Law and the Construction of Internal Labor Markets." *American Journal of Sociology* 992, (1993): 396–427.

Edelman, L. B., S. R. Fuller, and I. Mara-Drita. "Diversity Rhetoric and the Managerialization of Law." *American Journal of Sociology* 1066, (2001): 1589–1641.

Edelman, L. B. "Legal Ambiguity and Symbolic Structures: Organization Mediation of Civil Rights Law." *American Journal of Sociology* 6, (1992): 1531–1571.

Edelman, L. B., S. E. Abraham, and H. S. Erlanger. "Professional Construction of the Legal Environment: The Inflated Threat of Wrongful Discharge Doctrine." *Law and Society Review* 26, (1992): 47–83.

Edelman, L. B. "Legal Environments and Organizational Governance: The Expansion of Due Process of the American Workplace." *American Journal of Sociology* 95, (1990): 1401–1440.

Edwards, R. C. *The Contested Terrain: The Transformation of the Workplace in the Twentieth Century.* New York: Basic Books, 1977.

Galaskiewicz, J. *Social Organization of an Urban Grants Economy.* Orlando, FL: Academic Press, 1985.

Hall, R., J. Clark, P. Giordano, P. Johnson, and M. Van Roekel. "Patterns of Interorganizational Relationships." *Administrative Science Quarterly* 22, (September 1977): 457–474.

Hall, R. H. *Organizations: Structures, Process and Outcomes* 7th ed. New Jersey: Prentice Hall, 1999.

Heckman, J. and B. Payner. "Determining the Impact of Federal Antidiscrimination Policy on the Economic Status of Blacks: A Study of South Carolina." *American Economic Review* 79, (1989): 138–177.

Heidrick and Struggles. "The New Diversity: Women and Minorities on Corporate Boards." Heidrick and Struggles: Chicago, Illinois, 1993.

Herring, C. and S. Collins. *Retreat from Equal Opportunity? The Case of Affirmative Action.* In *The Bubbling Cauldron*, ed. M. P. Smith and J. Feagin (Minneapolis: University of Minnesota Press, 1995).

Information Technology Association of America. *Building a 21st Century Information Technology Workforce.* (Arlington, VA: Information Technology Association of America, 2001).

Information Technology Association of America. *Help Wanted: 1998: A Call for Collaborative Action for the New Millennium.* (Arlington, VA: Information Technology Association of America, 1998).

Jacoby, R. "The Myth of Multiculturalism." *New Left Review* 208, (1994): 121–126.

Joskow, P. L. "Vertical Integration and Long-Term Contracts: The Case of Coal-Burning Electric Generating Plants." *Journal of Law, Economics, and Organization* 1, (1985): 33–80.

Kahn, R. L. and Cannell, C. F. *The Dynamics of Interviewing: Theories, Techniques, and Cases.* New York: Wiley, 1957.

Kanter, R. *Men and Women of the Corporation.* New York: Basic Books, 1977.

Katz, D. and R. L. Kahn. *The Social Psychology of Organizations.* John Wiley and Sons, Inc: New York. 1966.

Lincoln, J. R. and K. McBride. "Resources, Homophily, and Dependence Organizational Attributes and Asymmetric Ties in Human Service Networks." *Social Science Research* 14, (1985): 1–30.

Loden, M. *Implementing Diversity.* New York: McGraw-Hill, 1996.
Loden, M. and J. B. Rosener. *Workforce America: Managing Employee Diversity as a Vital Resource.* Homewood, IL: Business One Irwin, 1991.

Lincoln, Y. and E. Guba. *Naturalistic Inquiry.* Thousand Oaks, CA: Sage Publications, 1985.

Lynch, F. R. *The Diversity Machine: The Drive to Change the "White Male Workplace."* New York: The Free Press, 1997.

Marshall, C. and G. Rossman. *Designing Qualitative Research* 2nd ed. Newbury Park, CA: Sage Publications, 1995.

Meyer, J. and B. Rowen. "Institutionalized Organizations: Formal Structure as Myth and Ceremony." *American Journal of Sociology* 83, (1977): 340–365.

Meyer, J. W. and W. R. Scott. *Organizational Environments: Ritual and Rationality*. Beverly Hills, CA: Sage Publications, 1983.

Mueller, N. L. "Wisconsin Power and Light's Model Diversity Program." *Training and Development* 50, no. 3 (1996): 57–60.

National Research Council. *Building a Workforce for the Information Economy*. (Washington, D.C.: National Research Council, 2001).

National Science Board. *Science and Engineering Indicators: 1996*. (Washington, D.C.: Government Printing Office, 1996).

National Science Foundation. *Women, Minorities, and Persons with Disabilities in Science and Engineering*. (Washington D.C.: National Science Foundation, 2000).

Norton, J. R. and R. Fox. *The Change Equation: Capitalizing on Diversity for Effective Organizational Change*. Washington, D.C.: American Psychological Association, 1997.

Pfeffer, J. and G. R. Salancik. *The External Control of Organizations: A Resource Dependence Perspective*. New York: Harper and Row, 1978.

Pennings, J. W. "Work Value Systems of White Collar Workers." *Administrative Science Quarterly* 15, (1979): 397–405.

Purcell, T. V. *Blue Collar Man: Patterns of Dual Allegiance in Industry*. Cambridge, MA: Harvard University Press, 1960.

Salzman, J. "Labor Rights, Globalization, and Institutions: The Role and Influence of the Organization for Economic Cooperation and

Development." *Michigan Journal of International Law* 21, (2000): 769–848.

Selznick, P. *Leadership in Administration: A Sociological Interpretation.* Berkeley: University of California Press, 1956.

Stinchombe, A. L. *Social Structure and Organizations.* In *Handbook of Organizations,* ed. J. G. March. Chicago: Rand McNally, 1965.

Tatum, B. D. *Why Are All the Black Kids Sitting Together in the Cafeteria?* New York: Basic Books, 2003.

Thomas, D. *Mentoring and Diversity in Organizations: Importance of Race and Gender in Work Relationships.* In *Workplace Diversity Issues and Perspectives,* ed. A. Daly (Washington, D.C.: National Association of Social Workers, 1998), 281–292.

Thomas, D. *Breaking Through: The Making of Minority Executives in Corporate America.* Cambridge, MA: Harvard Business School Press, 1999.

Thomas, R. R. *Redefining Diversity.* New York: American Management Association, 1994.

Tung, R. L. "Managing *Cross-National and Intra-National Diversity.*" *Human Resource Management Journal* 32, no. 4 (1993): 461–477.

Uri, N. D. and Mixon, W. J., Jr. "Effects of U.S. Affirmative Action Programs on Women's Employment." *Journal of Policy Modeling* 13, no. 3; 367–382.

U. S. Department of Commerce, Bureau of Labor Statistics. *Occupational Outlook Quarterly.* (Washington, D.C.: U. S. Department of Commerce, Bureau of Labor Statistics, Fall 1998).

U. S. Department of Education, National Center for Education Statistics. *Degrees and Other Awards Survey.* (Washington, D.C.: U. S. Department of Education, National Center for Education Statistics, 1998).

U. S. Department of Education, National Center for Education Statistics. *Digest of Education Statistics.* (Washington, D.C.: U. S. Department of Education, National Center for Education Statistics, 2000).

U. S. Department of Education, National Center for Education Statistics. *IPEDS Completion Survey.* (Washington, D.C.: U. S. Department of Education, National Center for Education Statistics, 1998).

U. S. National Science Board. *Undergraduate Science, Mathematics and Engineering Education.* (Washington, D.C.: U. S. National Science Board, 1997).

Wheeler, M. *Diversity Training.* The Conference Board, Research Report Number 1083-94RR. New York: Conference Board, 1994.

Whyte, W. F. *Learning from the Field: A Guide from Experience.* Beverly Hills, CA: Sage Publications, 1984.

Winterle, M. *Workforce Diversity: Corporate Challenges, Corporate Responses.* The Conference Board, Research Report Number 1013. New York: Conference Board, 1992.

Wood, P. W. *Diversity: The Invention of a Concept.* San Francisco: Encounter Books, 2003.

Yakura, E. K. *EEO Law and Managing Diversity.* In *Managing Diversity: Human Resources Strategies for Transforming the Workplace*, ed. E. E. Kossek and S. A. Lobel (Oxford, UK: Blackwell Publishers, 1996).

Index

CPSIA information can be obtained at www.ICGtesting.com
Printed in the USA
BVOW031827301111

277243BV00007B/116/P